W9-BCY-083

Taking Care of Myself

A Hygiene, Puberty and Personal Curriculum for Young People with Autism.

By Mary J. Wrobel
with contributions by Patricia Rielly

Taking Care of Myself

All marketing and publishing rights guaranteed to and reserved by

721 W. Abram Street
Arlington, Texas 76013
800-489-0727
817-277-0727
817-277-2270 (fax)
E-mail: info@FHautism.com
www.FHautism.com

Printed in the United States of America

Cataloging in Publications Data is available from the Library of Congress.

ISBN   1-885477-94-5

Acknowledgements

I don't claim to be an expert on growth and puberty. I'm fortunate, however, to know a number of school nurses, parents and teachers who have given me a wealth of information during the past several years, all of which has contributed to the stories and information presented in this curriculum. I want to thank Patricia Rielly especially, for sharing her knowledge, ideas and expertise for this curriculum. If it weren't for Pat's support, it's not likely this book would have been written.

I could not have created these materials without the help of a dedicated staff of assistants, who made the books and activities to be used with students. Special thanks to Bethany Hendricks for making and organizing the curriculum kits. Thanks also to John Cameron, Kelly Anderson and Cissy Sullivan.

Table of Contents

Unit 1 Hygiene 1

Unit 2 Health 57

Introduction

People with autism spectrum disorders typically have a difficult time understanding most verbal information presented to them. The reasons may vary from limited vocabulary comprehension or difficulty processing auditory information to poor problem solving skills and the inability to appropriately interact with others and understand social rules. Many such autism spectrum individuals need information presented in a clear, simple way at their level of comprehension. Social rules and expectations are typically a mystery to them. In fact most individuals with autism and related disabilities don't model others successfully and aren't able to figure out what they should do by following the examples of others. So the rules and information that they need to understand and follow must be explained in simple, precise detail.

Several years ago a school nurse and colleague of mine asked for my assistance in teaching the district mandated sex education curriculum to a population of autistic students. She was having difficulty teaching the required curriculum to these special needs students and didn't feel that it met their needs. From that starting point I began to develop the curriculum presented in this book. With the help of my colleague, Patricia Rielly, I devised a new way to address issues of hygiene, health, modesty, growth and development, menstruation, touching, personal safety, and masturbation. I feel these units cover essential information students with autism and other disabilities will need to lead healthy and safe lives.

Students from the ages of five to adult can benefit from some, or all, of this curriculum. However, some of the stories and activities in this book would not be appropriate for young students, particularly the curriculum and instruction for puberty. Young students can benefit from learning some of the hygiene and self-care skills such as using the toilet, brushing teeth and washing hands. I encourage parents and teachers to begin teaching these necessary hygiene and self-care skills when students are perhaps as young as three. Teaching these skills early, with the expectation of independence, helps establish appropriate self-care routines.

The stories and activities in this curriculum are designed for students having a variety of disabilities. The vocabulary is simple, but specific. The activities are presented with suggestions for modifications as well as examples of visual cues to encourage comprehension of the subject matter.

Examples of communication aids and assistive technology are shown throughout this booklet as a means of allowing students to comprehend and communicate more effectively. A variety of voice output devices as well as low or no-tech options are discussed and presented.

The purpose of this book is to teach students with autism and other disabilities the necessary information and skills they need to learn to live safe, healthy lives as independently as they are physically and mentally capable of. The goals of this curricular program are to promote independence, instill personal safety and reduce fear and confusion.

How to Use This Book

The curriculum in this book is divided into seven units presented in a somewhat natural progression: Hygiene, Health, Modesty, Growth and Development, Menstruation, Touching and Personal Safety, and Masturbation. Unlike the typical sex education curriculum presented to most normally developed students, this curriculum does not include information regarding sexual intercourse, reproduction, sexually transmitted diseases or birth control. This curriculum was specifically designed to address the health and safety needs of students with autism spectrum disorders. Students ages five through 18 are the target population, although older students and young adults may also benefit from this instruction. As students become young adults, you may need to supplement this curriculum with a more extensive sex education curriculum.

With an emphasis on made-up stories and activities, the curriculum is designed primarily for students who are visually strong and capable of some physical manipulation of items. The information is written using simple, concrete vocabulary aimed at students who are cognitively low, but also useful to higher functioning individuals. The text is designed to be divided into smaller, specific books identified by topic with some personalized for individuals and others constructed more generically for group instruction. Examples of story layouts and individual books appear throughout this booklet.

Many of the stories are written similar to the Social Stories™ style as employed by author Carol Gray. As with Social Stories™, some of these stories are about social situations and use descriptive, directive, and persuasive sentences as well as many affirmative statements. Because of the nature of the information presented, I also use some absolutes such as never and always to teach important rules about touching and safety. Although I try to end each topic with a positive, affirmative statement, some of the stories discuss inappropriate behavior and use strong language to explain what not to do.

You will notice that the stories in this booklet are written using a variety of styles from first person (I, me, my) to second person (you) and even third person (he, she, they). Sometimes a story is written from one point of view, but most have a variety of styles and points of view. The reason for this is to illustrate the variety of ways you can present each story or activity, and most importantly, to help each student understand and identify with specific concepts or lessons. Some students are confused by pronouns and may not relate to them. In those cases, you may want to use the student's first name in a story or activity. If a student is capable of reading the information, even with support, you may want to write the story in the first person style. I typically write stories for younger students this way, or use their first names. Stories for older students, or potentially upsetting stories, may be written in the third person. Regardless of how a story is written, the important point is that the student should understand the information presented and relate it to him or herself.

Addressing Communication and Language Needs

Language and comprehension is typically the most challenging skill for people with autism spectrum disorders. This is also true for higher language functioning ASD populations, such as individuals with Asperger's Syndrome. In order to teach any curriculum, which requires comprehension of information and appropriate responses on the part of each student, individual communication needs must be taken into account and met. As such, examples of various communication accommodations are pictured and discussed throughout this booklet.

Individuals with autism are often visually strong and in most cases need visual supports, such as pictures and written language, to understand information presented. Likewise, many ASD individuals are non-verbal or have limited verbal skills and may require voice output devices or picture communication boards to communicate.

Pictures and other visual supports may enhance comprehension of this curriculum. A variety of visual and tactile aids may be used: objects, photos, colored or black and white line drawings, and written language. Obviously, the level of ability and needs will vary from student to student. Some students can understand and use abstract pictures or line drawings for communicative needs, while others will require actual pictures. The Boardmaker Picture Communication Symbols manufactured by the Mayer-Johnson Company, and the Picture It/Pix Writer symbols produced by Slater Software, Inc. are good sources for abstract line drawings suitable for this curriculum. If a student is unable to understand abstract pictures, the Attainment Company produces many realistic line drawings which address health, hygiene and puberty topics. Some students may need actual photographs to illustrate the materials in this curriculum. Aside from taking pictures of actual items and places, instructors may look to a resource like the Picture This... software manufactured by Silver Lining Multimedia, Inc. which has many useful health, hygiene and self-care pictures which may be useful for instruction.

The quantity of pictures on a communication board or voice out-put device is also a consideration. While some students can handle an overlay with several pictures and varied language functions, such as requests, comments, protests/refusals, etc., other students may need few picture choices and limited language functions. When making visual and verbal supports for teaching this curriculum, determine the specific needs of a student or group of students, and decide how the student(s) will use the communicative supports.

Using the Computer with this Curriculum

Many students with autism as well as other learning differences are motivated to learn using computers. With the variety of interesting and fun software products on the market to meet the needs of various learning styles, computers are a natural curriculum aid. A computer's ability to catch and hold a student's attention and give audio and visual information, often simultaneously, allows for more learning opportunities.

Much of the curriculum included in this booklet can be easily used with a variety of computer software programs. The various stories may be written and illustrated on computer using standard word processors, or talking word processors, such as Write Outloud (Don Johnston Inc.). Students can create the stories, with the help of an adult, and respond to the information generated. Picture programs such as Boardmaker (Mayer-Johnson Company), Picture It and PixWriter both from Slater Software, Inc., and Picture This…(Silver Lining Multimedia, Inc.) may help illustrate the information. Not only do the pictures stimulate interest, they often increase student comprehension of the text.

Getting Started with this Curriculum

When should you start teaching this curriculum? It may be appropriate to begin teaching some basic health and hygiene instruction to young students, even as early as kindergarten. This will be especially important if parents are having difficulty establishing independent hygiene routines at home, such as toileting and hand washing. As students grow older, basic self-care skills become even more important as their hygiene needs change and modesty becomes essential. I typically teach hygiene skills to very young students and gradually add health and modesty instruction each year. In the public school environment, I recommend starting puberty instruction in the fourth grade and expanding on that curriculum each year, as students get older or as needed.

It's important to explain your curriculum to parents and solicit their input before you implement this program. Parents can offer insights about the health and hygiene routines they have at home, which you may want to continue or supplement at school. Furthermore, parents may have hygiene needs and priorities for their children, which you may need to address at school. I have found that most parents want to know how to teach their children these essential skills and will work with school personnel to aid in teaching these skills consistently.

Not everything in this curriculum is necessary for all students, but most of this information is important and it may be difficult, if not impossible for one person to teach all of it. It may be necessary and beneficial to divide the curricular instruction among school staff members, as well as parents. Seek the assistance of school nurses, social workers, school psychologists, instructional assistants, speech-language pathologists, classroom teachers and parents to help address various skills or specific topics. Consider teaching this curriculum throughout the school year, with periodic reviews of learned skills.

I further recommend segregating and instructing students by gender when teaching this curriculum, especially when teaching about puberty. It is often difficult enough to teach the information that each student needs to know, without adding information that is unrelated to their own growth and development. For example, teaching about the specific growth and development of the female gender may just confuse your male students.

Opposite gender instruction for most students with disabilities is typically unnecessary until students are in high school or older.

Certain curricular skills and topics, such as masturbation and menstruation should be taught one-on-one with students in a segregated setting. In most cases, it may be necessary to discuss these sensitive topics with parents and students prior to instruction. If possible, same gender instruction such as female to female and male to male is recommended.

Practice and repeated presentation of the curriculum may be necessary for mastery. This instruction can be incorporated into a student's yearly curriculum and the information and activities presented at various times throughout the school year. Examples of modifications and ways to instruct students are illustrated and discussed throughout this booklet.

Steps for Developing a Successful Program

1. Gather Information

- Parent input: What skills does the student(s) demonstrate, or not demonstrate at home? What is a priority for the parent? What is the student demonstrating at school?

- What is the language comprehension level of the student(s)? What is the cognitive ability?

- What is the learning style of the student(s)?

2. Student Participation

- What materials and assistive technology will be needed?

- What prompts and cues will be needed?

- How will the student(s) respond?

3. Assess the Environment

- Is small group or individual instruction appropriate?

- What are the environmental considerations? (such as auditory, tactile and visual stimuli)

- What can be sent home for instruction? What needs to be instructed at school?

4. Consider Objectives

- How will this curriculum be included in the student's IEP (Individualized Educational Plan)?

- How will you generate the student's individual learning plan with parents? (see COACH, Choosing Options and Accommodations for Children in references)

- How is this curriculum supported by your state's standards? (Some states require adherence to state standards).

5. Implementation

- How will you prioritize and order this curriculum for your student(s)?

- Who will teach this curriculum? (classroom teacher/ school nurse/ social worker/speech-language pathologist/ instructional aid/ parent/ a team of instructors) How will you divide the curriculum for instruction?

- What is the schedule of instruction? (Seasonally, included in weekly or daily curriculums)

6. Evaluation

- How will you evaluate student progress? (Checklists, demonstration of skills, various data collection)

- How will you obtain parent feedback?

- How will you determine independent carryover of skills at school and home?

Voice Output Devices

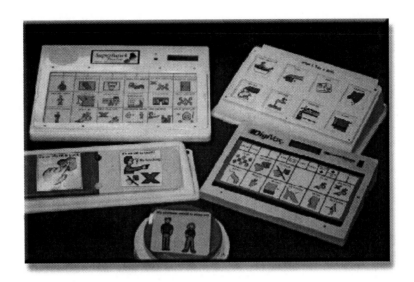

Voice output devices allow students who have limited verbal ability to respond appropriately to questions and take part in discussions. The above pictured devices (clockwise from top left: Superhawk, Cheaptalk, Digivox2, Big Mack, and Rocker Switch) have overlays ranging from 18 different voice output responses (Superhawk, as shown) to 1 voice output response (Big Mack). You can choose the device used according the needs and abilities of the student and the types of responses that you want given.

Note: the Superhawk and Digivox2 are capable of having up to 36 responses on a single overlay.

HYGIENE

Independent hygiene skills promote physical well being and social acceptance

 What's Dirty

 Washing My Hands

 Taking Care of My Body

 We Need to Take a Bath or Shower

 I Can Take a Bath

 I Wash My Hair with Shampoo

 I Can Take a Shower by Myself

 We Brush Our Teeth

 Sometimes I Need a Haircut

 I Need to Comb and Brush My Hair

 Blowing My Nose

 Picking My Nose

 Alex Uses the Toilet

 I Use the Bathroom at School

 Using Toilet Paper

Teaching Hygiene

Most students with disabilities do not independently take care of all their personal hygiene needs. Unfortunately, if someone never learns or is incapable of taking care of their own bathing and dressing, then they will always be dependent on others, such as family members or paid staff, to do those necessary jobs. Not only is this a daily, time-consuming job for others to perform, but it could also result in possible molestation or abuse, at some point, on the part of the dependent person. I believe it is essential that all people with disabilities learn to take care of their personal hygiene needs as independently as possible. Students should be taught most hygiene and self-care skills before puberty, and in most cases on a continuing basis as a part of their daily learning curriculum.

Learning independent hygiene skills is increasingly important as students become older because it teaches them self-care, modesty and responsibility. Puberty is also a time when cleanliness becomes a contributing factor to both their self-esteem and health.

Begin teaching the basics of daily cleaning routines such as baths or showers, shampooing, brushing teeth, blowing the nose, washing hands, and combing hair. Later, add using deodorant, dressing oneself in clean clothes, and specific hygiene skills according to gender and individual needs. Use stories and pictures to illustrate each skill. There should be plenty of opportunity to practice the skills at school or home, when appropriate.

It is necessary to work closely with parents to establish routines and strive for independence at home. It may be impossible to practice certain skills at school, such as bathing and shampooing. Therefore, parents may need some instruction on the importance of teaching their children these skills at home and allowing the students daily independent practice of their self-care skills.

One way to do this is to create a hygiene book for an individual student. The book could show products that the child uses, step by step instructions or schedules to follow, and photos of the child independently carrying out hygiene routines. Encourage students to create their own books and choose pictures of the hygiene products they want to include.

The hygiene book is about them, and can become a source of pride for a student as well as a reminder of what they need to do to take care of their hygiene. I further recommend creating home schedules for hygiene routines with step-by-step progressions for each hygiene task.

Additional activities could include: sequencing photo cards which illustrate a skill, such as toothbrushing, fill-in the-blank worksheets for each hygiene topic, "what's wrong?" photo cards to generate problem solving and determine comprehension, mini response stories in which students read and velcro on the appropriate response, and question & answer cards which can be used with a group or an individual student. Several examples of these activities are included in this unit.

Obviously, not all students will be able to be completely independent in their hygiene skills. The goal here is to help them be as independent as possible. For some students it may take years to teach independent self-care and good hygiene skills. It is never too early or too late to start. This may become an important life-long goal.

Some students may understand why good hygiene and self-care is important, but other students may never understand why we need to clean ourselves every day. The important thing is that students get into a routine of appropriate, daily hygiene skills even if they can't understand why we need to do it.

The following stories and activities in this unit will help teach students with autism and other disabilities necessary hygiene skills which will allow them to be more independent and responsible for their self-care.

The goals and anticipated progression of skills for this unit:

- The student will tolerate specific hygiene tasks (i.e: hand washing, toothbrushing, nose blowing, toileting.)

- The student will participate in basic hygiene routines with support.

- The student will demonstrate the steps of specific hygiene routines with support.

- The student will independently perform specific hygiene skills with prompts.

- The student will initiate basic hygiene routines at home as well as at school.

- The student will effectively and appropriately perform specific hygiene skills on his/her own in various environments.

Many students are told their hands are dirty, or something is dirty, and they shouldn't touch dirty things. But the concept of 'dirty' is often a difficult one for students to understand. This story explains what things are typically dirty and why we need to wash our hands after touching dirty things. It also introduces the concept of germs, as something dirty that can make us sick but that we can't see.

↳ Dirty things are full of dirt and germs.

↳ Lots of things are dirty. Sometimes I can see the dirt. But sometimes the dirt and germs are there and I can't see them.

↳ Dirt and germs can make me and other people sick. Dirt and germs are not good for my body.

↳ Almost everything is dirty sometimes, but some things are dirty all the time. Floors, toilets, mud, dirt, bugs, garbage, snot from noses, pee and poop are always dirty.

↳ I must not eat anything dirty, or put anything dirty in my mouth. Dirty things are full of germs and can make me sick.

- My hands are often dirty because my hands touch many dirty things. Even when my hands don't look dirty, they will be dirty with germs if I touch something that's dirty.

- I need to wash my hands every day with soap and water to take off the dirt and germs. I should wash my hands every time I touch something dirty.

- I will remember that many things are dirty and full of germs. Dirt and germs can make me sick.

I need to wash my hands with soap and water whenever I touch dirty things.

The Picture Communication Symbols copyright 1981-2002, Mayer-Johnson, Inc. Used with permission.

Students can learn to identify clean and dirty using actual pictures as well as abstract Boardmaker pictures. Using velcro picture responses and voice output devices provide appropriate ways for students to respond.

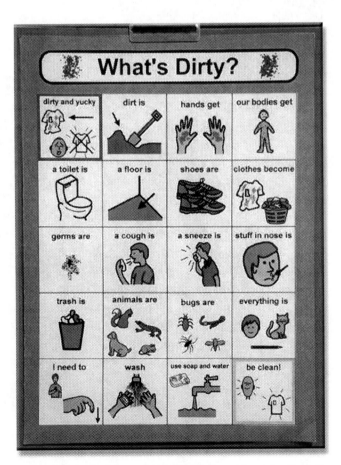

The Picture Communication Symbols copyright 1981-2002, Mayer-Johnson, Inc. Used with permission.

Learning to wash hands properly with soap and water is a hygiene routine we often take for granted. Unless it is taught appropriately and students learn to wash hands routinely throughout the day, steps are likely to be missed and students will not automatically wash hands when they should.

Washing My Hands

↪ I need to wash my hands every day.

↪ My hands touch many things each day and get dirty. Dirty hands can sometimes make me sick.

↪ I need to wash my hands with soap and water so they will be clean.

↪ I need to wash my hands before I eat and touch food.

↪ I need to wash my hands after I blow and wipe my nose.

↪ I need to wash my hands after I use the toilet.

↪ I need to wash my hands many times each day.

➪ I will wash my hands with soap and water. First I put soap on my hands and rub them gently. I need to get the soap all over my fingers and hands.

➪ Then I rinse off my hands with warm, clean water and dry them with a clean towel.

➪ Now my hands will be clean for awhile. But soon my hands will get dirty and I'll need to wash them again.

➪ I will remember to wash my hands every day. I will do a good job washing my hands with soap and water.

 I will remember to wash my hands every day. I will do a good job washing my hands with soap and water.

This is a story which can be used as an introduction to basic hygiene skills or as a review of the basic hygiene skills a student has learned. The story becomes a test of individual comprehension when the student is asked to find an appropriate picture for each statement presented.

Taking Care of My Body

⇨ I need to take care of my body.

⇨ I need to clean my body every day.

⇨ I need to dress myself.

⇨ I need to eat good foods.

⇨ I need to look neat and be clean.

⇨ When I do a good job taking care of my body, I feel happy, comfortable and proud.

⇨ Every day I wash my face and hands.

⇨ Every day I brush my teeth.

⇨ Every day I comb my hair.

 Every day I wash myself.

 Every day I put on comfortable, clean clothing.

 Every day I need to eat good, nutritious food.

I will do a good job taking care of my body. I will be healthy and happy.

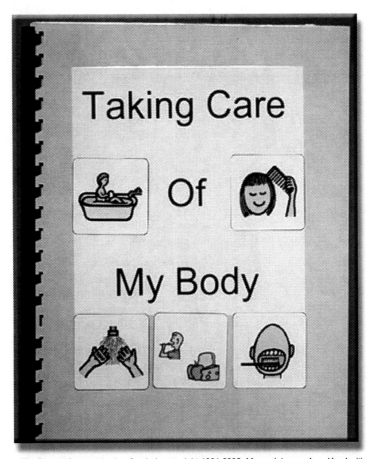

The following story introduces the concept of independent, daily bathing. This is a good story to send home. Be sure to include photos or line-drawing pictures with each page. Parents can read the story with their child and then help the child follow the necessary steps and solve problems as needed. Point to the pictures as you read the story to help the student comprehend the information. Eventually we want all students to learn to bathe themselves.

We Need To Take A Bath Or Shower

↳ We need to wash our bodies every day.

↳ Most people take a bath or shower to wash their bodies.

↳ People usually take a bath or shower in the morning or before bedtime.

↳ Our bodies become dirty and sweaty every day. Sometimes our bodies smell stinky. It's important to take a bath or shower to clean ourselves and smell nice.

↳ When I take a bath or shower I need to use clean, warm water and soap. I need to wash every part of my body with soap and then rinse myself off with clean, warm water. I can use a wash cloth or scrubbie when I wash myself.

↳

➭ I will get my hair wet and wash my hair with shampoo. I will put a little shampoo on my head and lather all my hair. Then I will rinse my hair until all the shampoo is out.

➭ When I'm finished washing myself and rinsing, I'll get out of the shower or bath and dry myself off with a towel.

➭ I need to get dressed in clean underwear and clothing. If I'm going to bed I need to put on clean pajamas.

 I will do a good job of washing myself every day.

This is a sequence folder activity in which the student needs to read or have dictated the numbered steps in the folder, then find the appropriate picture to go with each step. This is a helpful activity because it teaches the step by step sequence of taking a bath. It also serves as an independent demonstration by a student of the bath process. Because this activity uses velcroed picture responses for each step, non-verbal students and even non-readers can participate.

A number of folder activities for other hygiene skills can be created using this format.

I Can Take A Bath

Folder activity steps

1 I fill the tub with warm water.

2 I take off all my clothes.

3 I get into the tub.

4 I wash my whole body with soap and water.

5 I rinse the soap off my body with warm water.

6 I get out of the bathtub.

7 I dry myself off with a towel.

8 I get dressed. I put on clean clothes.

9 I did a good job!

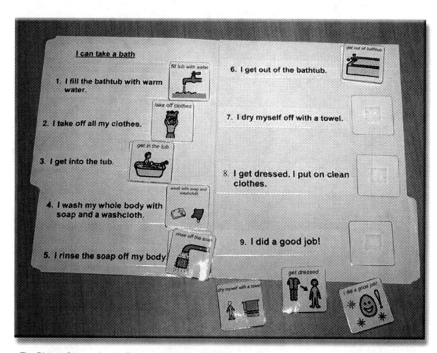

The Picture Communication Symbols copyright 1981-2002, Mayer-Johnson, Inc. Used with permission.

Learning to wash hair with shampoo or even to tolerate hair washing can be a problem because of soap/shampoo dripping down the face and possibly getting into the eyes. Many students, unfortunately, hate to have soap or water on their heads. It is helpful to find a shampoo that smells good and feels good to your child or student. Practice shampooing a doll's hair first or allow the child to shampoo mom or dad's hair. As with most hygiene skills, it may be necessary to start slow and be persistent. Once children accept shampooing as a part of a hygiene routine, they will be more ready to learn to shampoo on their own.

I Wash My Hair with Shampoo

⤷ My hair can get dirty, greasy and smell bad. Sometimes I need to wash my hair.

⤷ Shampoo will clean my hair and make my hair smell nice.

⤷ Mommy or Daddy will help me shampoo my hair.

⤷ When I take a bath or shower I will get my hair all wet and then put a small amount of hampoo on my head.

⤷ I will lather the shampoo into my hair and cover all my hair with shampoo. The shampoo will feel soapy and sudsy. The shampoo will smell nice.

- I will try not to get the shampoo in my eyes. If I do, shampoo may sting my eyes. I can keep my eyes shut and wipe my eyes with a wash cloth.

- If the shampoo gets in my eyes I will be okay. Mommy will help me wipe it out and I will feel better soon.

- I need to rinse off the shampoo with clean, warm water. Mommy or Daddy will help me rinse all the shampoo out of my hair.

- Now my hair is nice and clean. Mommy or Daddy will help me comb and dry my hair.

 I will do a good job of shampooing my hair. I like to have clean, pretty hair.

At some point, it becomes important to let children bathe themselves. It's not only important for their self-esteem, but also for practical reasons and modesty. Some children will be ready to bathe themselves at 10 or 11 years old. Parents can usually tell when a child is able to bathe himself without assistance. Then, it's important to encourage independent bathing. I recommend that students be bathing themselves at least by the time they reach puberty, if they are physically and mentally capable of it. I also recommend to parents that they teach children to shower as a means of independent bathing. It is often quicker, easier and more hygienic than taking a bath. Most adults shower, and students may need to shower in high school, so learning to shower can be an important step toward independent, life-long bathing.

I Can Take A Shower By Myself

↳ I am a big (boy/girl). I know how to take a shower.

↳ Mom and Dad say I can take a shower by myself.

↳ It's okay to take a shower by myself. I'm a big (boy/girl) and I need privacy when I take a shower.

↳ I know what to do when I take a shower.

↳ I can do all the things by myself. Mom or Dad can remind me about what to do if I forget.

↳ When I'm ready to take a shower, I go into the bathroom and close the door. I don't want people to see me undressing for my shower.

1. First, I close the shower curtain. It's important that the shower curtain is inside the tub. When the curtain is inside the shower tub, water won't get on the floor.

2. I reach in and turn on the faucet. I wait until the water feels nice and warm. I don't want very hot water and I don't want cold water for my shower.

3. When the water feels warm to me, I will turn on the shower.

4. I will take off all my clothes before getting into the shower. I will close the shower curtain when I step into the tub (or shower stall).

5. I will be sure I have my washcloth, soap and shampoo with me in the shower.

6. I will get all wet with warm water. I will get my face and hair wet too.

7. I will take the washcloth and soap and wash my face, neck and ears.

8. I will wash my arms, underarms, chest and tummy with soap.

9. I will wash my legs, back and feet with soap.

10. I will wash my bottom and between my legs with soap.

11. I will rinse off all the soap with warm water.

12. Sometimes, I will wash my hair when I take a shower. I will pour a small amount of shampoo into one hand.
Then I will lather the shampoo into my hair with both hands. I will be careful not to get any shampoo into my eyes.

13. After my hair is nice and soapy, I will rinse off the shampoo. Sometimes it takes a while to get all the shampoo out of my hair. I will feel my hair to be sure all the shampoo is out.

14. When the shampoo is rinsed out of my hair, and all the soap is rinsed off my body, I can turn off the water.

15. After I turn off the water, I will carefully step out of the shower and dry myself off with a towel.

16. When I'm all dry, I will put on clean clothes or pajamas.

When I'm dressed, I can open the bathroom door and leave. I did a great job taking a shower!

Many children with autism have a hard time tolerating and learning tooth brushing. Parents often tell me their children will tolerate other hygiene skills but brushing teeth is a battle. I tell parents to begin the toothbrushing routine as early as possible and to take very small steps. Our students typically brush their teeth every day after lunch at school to reinforce the routine of toothbrushing and to increase their tolerance and independent skills.

We Brush Our Teeth

⮡ People brush their teeth to keep them clean and healthy.

⮡ Everyone needs to brush their teeth.

⮡ I should brush my teeth after I eat. I can brush my teeth after breakfast, snack, lunch and dinner. I will brush my teeth before I go to bed.

⮡ I need to brush my teeth two or three times a day so my teeth will be clean and healthy.

⮡ Brushing my teeth keeps my teeth clean, and gives me clean-smelling breath.

⮡ Brushing my teeth will also prevent cavities. I don't want cavities! Cavities are bad for my teeth. Cavities can make my teeth hurt.

⇨ I brush my teeth at the sink. I will need my toothbrush, toothpaste and water.

⇨ First, I get my toothbrush. I can only brush my teeth with my toothbrush.

⇨ Now I'm ready for toothpaste. I pick up the toothpaste and take off the cap.

⇨ I squeeze just a little bit of toothpaste onto my toothbrush. I will be careful not to let any toothpaste spill.

⇨ I put the cap back on the toothpaste.

⇨ I put the toothbrush with toothpaste into my mouth. The toothpaste may taste like mint or cinnamon, or maybe even bubblegum.

⇨ The toothpaste tastes good but I don't eat or swallow the toothpaste. Toothpaste is not food!

➫ I move the toothbrush back and forth, up and down, on my teeth. I will be sure to brush all of my teeth.

➫ When I'm finished brushing, I take the toothbrush out and spit all of the toothpaste into the sink. I don't swallow the toothpaste.

➫ I rinse my mouth with water and spit again. I rinse off my toothbrush and put my toothbrush away.

➫ I'm finished brushing my teeth! My teeth are clean and healthy. I did a good job brushing my teeth.

 I will remember to brush my teeth every day. I will do a good job brushing all of my teeth.

The Picture Communication Symbols copyright 1981-2002, Mayer-Johnson, Inc. Used with permission.

You can create a variety of books, activities, worksheets, and overlays for each skill area to enhance learning and achieve maximum comprehension.

The Picture Communication Symbols copyright 1981-2002, Mayer-Johnson, Inc. Used with permission.

Creating cut and paste worksheets helps to reinforce skills with students and allows them to demonstrate what they know independently.

Haircuts and nailcare can be traumatic for students with autism and other learning differences. Many parents tell me they have to cut nails and hair while their child is sleeping, and sometimes even that doesn't work. Explaining what will happen during a haircut and addressing a child's fears will help to make the whole experience less traumatic. One mother gave me a tip for haircutting. She found giving her son a (small) haircut each Saturday night got him used to the routine and alleviated his fears. Furthermore, since she cut very little of his hair each week, he never looked dramatically different after each haircut. The following story can also be used for cutting fingernails by replacing the word "hair" with "fingernails" and "haircut" with "fingernail cut", etc.

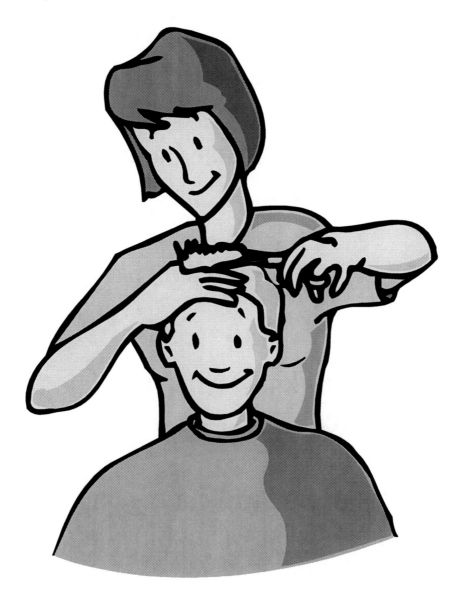

Sometimes I Need a Haircut

↳ Hair grows and grows. The hair on my head grows slowly until it is long.

↳ When my hair is too long I need to have a haircut.

↳ Everybody's hair grows. When hair grows too long it needs to be cut short again.

↳ Both kids and adults need haircuts when their hair grows too long.

↳ When my hair grows too long I will need a haircut.

↳ Mom or Dad will know when it's time for me to have a haircut.

↳ Maybe Mom or Dad will cut my hair. Maybe a barber or hair stylist will cut my hair.

↳ When I have a haircut I will sit quietly in the chair and wait for my hair to be cut. I will only need to wait a short time.

↳ Maybe I will be scared and worried about my haircut. But I know a haircut will be okay.

↳ A haircut doesn't hurt. Sometimes a haircut will tickle and feel strange, but it doesn't hurt to have a haircut.

↳ Maybe I won't like the way I look with a haircut. Maybe I will look different.

↳ It's okay to look different. I will get used to the way I look and soon my hair will grow long again.

↳ When my hair grows too long I know I will need another haircut. I will do a good job getting a haircut.

↳ I will look (handsome/pretty) with my new haircut. Having a haircut is okay.

We often forget the importance of simple hygiene skills such as combing and brushing hair. By learning this skill, students can begin to take responsibility for their own appearance. They can learn to check themselves in a mirror, and determine whether their hair needs combing or not. As with most personal hygiene skills, students can learn to be proud of their own achievements. Many parents report that combing or brushing hair is often a task that their children wouldn't think of doing for themselves. The sooner students begin to use a comb or brush, the better. Students should get into the routine of combing or brushing their hair every morning. They should face a mirror and watch themselves brushing their hair. This is a great way to teach them to check their own appearance. How do I look? Is my face clean? Is my hair neat and tidy? As with all skills, start small. Even if a child is simply going through the motions of brushing his or her hair, by instilling this routine they will eventually become better at combing and brushing with continued guidance.

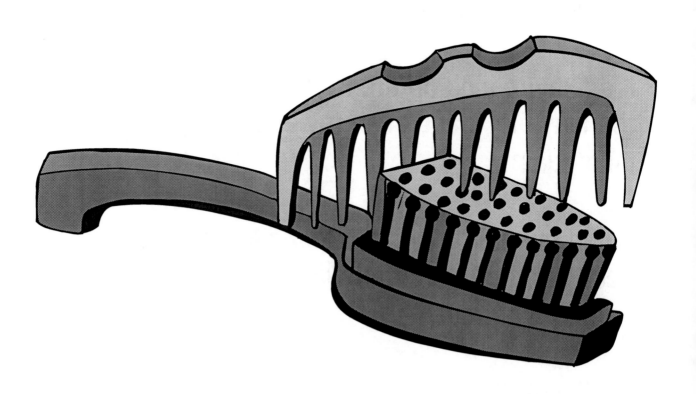

I Need to Comb and Brush My Hair

⇨ People use a comb or brush to help their hair stay neat and tidy.

⇨ I need to use a comb or brush everyday to keep my hair tidy and tangle-free.

⇨ After I wash my hair, and my hair is wet and tangled, I need to use a comb to gently comb out the tangles. Sometimes Mom or Dad will help me comb out the tangles in my hair.

⇨ Sometimes the air will dry my hair and sometimes Mom or Dad will blow dry my hair.

⇨ When my hair is dry I can use a comb or brush to make my hair look nice.

⇨ I should brush or comb my hair every morning before I go to school.

➪ Sometimes my hair will stay neat and tidy all day. But sometimes my hair will become tangled and messy and then I need to brush or comb it again.

➪ Sometimes it's hard to keep my hair tidy, and I need to comb it many times a day.

➪ I can check my hair in a mirror to see if I need to comb or brush it.

➪ If my hair is messy, I will gently comb or brush it. If I feel a tangle in my hair I will gently comb it out or ask an adult to help.

➪ I shouldn't pull hard with the comb or brush. Pulling hard may hurt and it could pull out some hair. I should comb or brush my hair gently.

➪ It's okay to comb or brush my hair in a bathroom, or my bedroom. But sometimes it's not okay to comb or brush my hair in other places.

➪ I should not comb or brush my hair around food.

 I want to have neat and tidy hair. I will do a good job combing and brushing my hair everyday.

Knowing how to correctly blow and wipe a nose is a skill many students with autism don't have. The reason they may pick their noses, wipe noses on sleeves and hands and allow their noses to run or drip is because they don't know how to blow and wipe them properly with a tissue. There are hygiene, sanitation and appropriate social issues associated with this skill.

Blowing My Nose

↳ Every day there is stuff in my nose.

↳ I need to blow and wipe my nose every day to get the snot out.

↳ When I am sick with a cold or runny nose, I need to blow and wipe my nose many times a day.

↳ Sometimes when I sneeze, lots of stuff will come out of my nose.

↳ I always need to blow and wipe my nose with a tissue.

↳ After I blow and wipe my nose, I throw away the tissue and wash my hands with soap and water.

↳

➼ The stuff in my nose is dirty and yucky. I must never eat the stuff in my nose. I must always wash my hands after I touch the stuff in my nose.

➼ To blow my nose, I lay the tissue over my nose and cover my nostrils.

➼ I cover one nostril with my finger and blow gently. Then I cover the other nostril with my finger and blow gently.

➼ I wipe my nose a little more and fold the tissue. I throw the tissue in the trash. Then, I wash my hands with soap and water.

➼ I can do a good job of blowing my nose. I will gently blow my nose every day to get the snot out.

 The stuff in my nose is dirty and yucky. I will remember to wash my hands after I blow my nose.

The following story is about nose-picking. This is often a problem for students with disabilities because they typically don't blow their noses well. If they are capable of picking their noses, they usually will, and often at the worse times and most inappropriate places. I have found that telling them not to pick their noses does not solve the problem. They'll do it anyway. So giving students the appropriate rules and restrictions for this behavior is the most practical and realistic approach. However, you don't necessarily want to teach a student to pick his/her nose, so if this isn't a behavior exhibited by a student, you might skip this story.

Picking My Nose

⇨ Sometimes, people pick their noses.

⇨ Sometimes, stuff gets stuck in my nose and I can't blow it out with a tissue. Then it's okay to pick my nose.

⇨ But picking my nose is dirty and yucky. I must use a tissue when I blow or pick my nose. I must wash my hands after I touch my nose.

⇨ People don't want to see me pick my nose. I don't pick my nose in front of people. When I need to, I will pick my nose in the bathroom.

⇨ I need to blow my nose first. If I can't get the stuff out of my nose, it is okay to gently remove it with my finger and a tissue. The stuff in my nose needs to go on a tissue.

↳ After I use a tissue with my nose, I will throw out the tissue and wash my hands with soap and water.

↳ Blowing, wiping and picking my nose is dirty. I must wash my hands after I touch my nose.

↳ The stuff in my nose is always dirty and yucky. I must never eat anything from my nose. It can make me sick. I must put the stuff from my nose into a tissue.

↳ I will only pick my nose when blowing my nose with a tissue doesn't work. I will not do it in front of other people.

↳ I will remember to use a tissue when I blow or pick my nose. If I have to pick my nose, I will do it in the bathroom and use a tissue. I will wash my hands after I touch my nose.

I will do a good job of taking care of my nose.

The following is a personalized story about using the toilet. The purpose of this story is to reduce fear and confusion, and establish an appropriate toileting routine. I recommend creating a personal story about using the toilet starring the individual student who is learning this routine. Stories may also be created for home use, with references to home toileting routines and individual needs. Always use the name of the individual student and include pictures of the actual bathrooms and other important materials used. It's also important to use the actual toileting words used by the student and family. Be sure to address any fears or problems the student may have regarding the whole procedure of toileting. And as always, use language the student will understand.

Alex Uses the Toilet

⇨ People use the toilet. Mommy and Daddy and all of my teachers use the toilet. Big boys and girls do a good job using the toilet. Alex is a big boy. Alex will do a good job using the toilet too.

⇨ Alex goes to the bathroom every day. Alex sits on the toilet at home and Alex sits on the toilet at school. Alex does a good job sitting on the toilet.

⇨ Alex will be okay in the bathroom. Alex will like going to the bathroom. When it's time to go to the bathroom, my teacher will say, "Time to go to the bathroom, Alex." Alex is ready to go to the bathroom.

⇨ Alex will do a good job walking to the bathroom. If Alex is upset he can say, "I'm upset, I'm scared!" It's okay to be upset and scared, but it's not okay to hurt others. Alex will use words and nice touches.

↳ My teachers help me use the toilet at school. My teachers need to wear rubber gloves to keep their hands clean. The rubber gloves look funny and I don't like them. But I know my teachers must wear them. The rubber gloves are okay. Alex will ignore the rubber gloves. Alex will do a good job with his teachers in the bathroom.

↳ When it's time to use the toilet, Alex takes off his pants and pull-ups all by himself. Now Alex is ready to sit on the toilet and go pee or poop. Good job, Alex!

↳ Sometimes when Alex sits on the toilet he will go pee. Sometimes when Alex sits on the toilet he will go poop. Sometimes when Alex sits on the toilet there will be no pee and no poop. That's okay. Alex does a good job sitting on the toilet and trying to go pee or poop.

↳ When Alex goes pee and poop in the toilet, he will get a special present. Sometimes Alex will get a treat. Sometimes Alex will get a toy. Alex will be proud and happy when he goes pee or poop in the toilet. Great job, Alex! Yeah!

↳

⇨ Sometimes Alex is worried about going pee or poop in the toilet. Alex worries about how it will feel. It's okay to be a little worried. Soon Alex will go pee and poop in the toilet and it will feel fine. Alex will be happy because he did a good job going pee and poop in the toilet and it feels fine.

⇨ When Alex is finished sitting on the toilet he will wipe himself with toilet paper and drop the toilet paper into the toilet. Alex will stand up, pull up his pull-ups and pull up his pants by himself. Alex will flush the toilet and wash his hands with soap and water. Good job using the bathroom, Alex!

When Alex goes pee and poop in the toilet, he will feel proud. Alex does a good job of using the toilet. Alex is a big boy when he goes pee and poop in the toilet. Yeah, Alex!

Learning to use the bathroom at school and in other places is an important, independent skill. Many young students with autism begin school not yet toilet trained. Sometimes it becomes the responsibility of a student's staff and teachers to teach appropriate toileting skills. The following is a generic bathroom story, which explains the step by step procedure for using a bathroom at school.

I Use the Bathroom at School

↳ I use the bathroom at school.

↳ I walk into the (girl's/boy's) bathroom.

↳ I go into the toilet stall (or the urinal) and shut the door.

↳ I pull down my pants.

↳ I pull down my underpants (pullups).

↳ I sit on the toilet. (I stand in front of the urinal.)

↳ I will pee and sometimes go poop in the toilet. (I hold my penis and pee into the urinal).

↳ I wipe my bottom with toilet paper and I drop the toilet paper into the toilet. (I gently shake my penis over the urinal.)

⇨ When I'm finished using the toilet (urinal) I flush it.

⇨ I pull up my underpants (pullups). I pull up my pants.

⇨ I walk to the sink and wash my hands with soap and water. I rinse my hands.

⇨ I dry my hands with a paper towel.

⇨ I'm finished using the bathroom at school. Now I go back to class.

 I did a good job of using the bathroom!

Using toilet paper appropriately and independently is an important step in toileting. We often take for granted that our students understand the use of toilet paper and can use toilet paper effectively and hygienically, but sometimes they need some extra coaching. The following story will help to teach why we use toilet paper and how to use it correctly.

↳ We use toilet paper after we pee or poop in the toilet.

↳ Toilet paper cleans and dries my bottom after I pee or poop in the toilet.

↳ I need to wipe my bottom and private areas with toilet paper to get the pee and poop off. I want my bottom to feel clean and dry.

↳ My bottom and private areas will feel better after I wipe myself with toilet paper.

↳ When I'm finished going in the toilet, I will pull off some toilet paper to wipe myself.

↳ Mom or Dad will show me how much to pull off.

↳ I will hold the toilet paper in one hand, and slowly wipe my bottom from the front to the back one time.

⇘ Then I need to drop the toilet paper in the toilet. After I wipe my bottom, the toilet paper must stay in the toilet.

⇘ Sometimes I may need some more toilet paper to wipe my bottom. It's okay to wipe again. When my bottom is wiped clean, I am finished using toilet paper.

⇘ Now I can pull up my underpants and my pants. My bottom will feel clean and dry.

⇘ Now I must wash my hands. I will always wash my hands after I finish wiping myself with toilet paper.

⇘ Now my bottom and my hands feel clean.

 I will do a good job of using toilet paper when I pee and poop in the toilet.

Creating Question-Answer Hygiene Cards

Question-answer cards are an effective tool for targeting specific topics. They can be used to discuss information, and review and evaluate student skills and knowledge. I typically create these cards in a flashcard format with the question on my side and the answer on the other. Visual cues such as actual or abstract pictures help to cue students.

Hygiene Question-Answer Cards:

1. Why do we need to wash our hands?

Answers: so we don't spread germs, to keep our hands clean, so we don't get sick, and to keep our bodies healthy.

2. Why do we take baths or showers?

Answers: to keep our bodies clean and healthy, to get germs and dirt off our body, and to smell nice.

3. Why do we need to brush our teeth?

Answers: for a clean mouth and teeth, for healthy teeth, for fresh breath, so we don't get cavities or a toothache, and to have short, easy visits to the dentist.

4. Why do we blow and wipe our noses with tissue?

Answers: to help dry up runny noses, to get the yucky stuff out, and to keep from spreading germs when we're sick with colds

HEALTH

Understanding and demonstrating good health practices promotes physical well being and essential life safety skills

 Being Healthy

 Eating Fruits & Vegetables

 I Sleep at Night

 Sometimes I Feel Sick

 I Feel Sick

 Sometimes I Have Pain

 Going to the Doctor

 Going to the Dentist

 Wearing a Bandage

 I Don't Touch Blood

 Taking Medicine

Teaching Health

Health and hygiene go hand in hand, since good hygiene is a big part of staying healthy. But the concepts of good and bad health are often too abstract for students with special needs to comprehend since there are so many factors involved: cleanliness, eating right, exercising and getting proper rest as well as dealing with sickness, injury and pain. The stories and activities in this unit address very basic health needs. You may need to create new stories as specific needs arise, but the materials in this unit will serve as a good starting point.

Pain and sickness are two essential concepts that all students need to understand and use. But, in more than twenty years spent working with students with autism, mental impairment and a variety of syndromes, I've found that one of the things these students typically have in common is an inability to react appropriately to either. Their reactions to pain may be as diverse and unusual as running, screaming, throwing things, withdrawing or demonstrating aggressive or self-stimulating behaviors. What these students typically don't do is seek adult help, explain that they are in pain, and show where their pain is. The same is often true for sickness. Unless there are obvious signs of sickness like fever or runny noses, adult caregivers may not know what's wrong. Some parents believe they can always tell when their children are sick or in pain, but even then, their analysis of the condition may not be completely accurate. And since they can't typically be with their school-age children all the time, it commonly falls to school personnel to make such judgments. When students react inconsistently or unusually to illness and discomfort, teachers and other staff members have a hard time determining the source of the problem.

I heard a story several years ago of a non-verbal student with autism who almost died of a ruptured appendix. He was in a residential placement and apparently began to act unusual. He withdrew from others and rocked frantically, possibly in an effort to calm himself. He refused to eat and aggressed toward those who approached him. It was not until his appendix ruptured and he exhibited a high fever that staff members were able to determine the seriousness of his condition. This was a potentially fatal situation and serves as a good example of why it's so important to teach our students to recognize pain and sickness and help them communicate to responsible adults when they are in physical distress.

Teaching these concepts can be difficult, however, and I have found it helpful to use situations involving minor pain and sickness as opportunities for helping students learn and demonstrate the proper responses. Practicing by using assistive technology and role playing with adults is also useful for reinforcing both the concepts and the appropriate responses.

The following stories and activities address a variety of health needs. Most of the material in this unit focuses on good health practices. Some stories specifically address emergency health concerns.

The goals and anticipated progression of skills for this unit:

- Student will demonstrate understanding of good health practices

- Student will tolerate and follow through on designated, appropriate health practices

- Student will tolerate eating some healthy foods

- Student will understand the concept of sickness

- Student will understand the term "pain"

- Student will demonstrate the appropriate responses to sickness (i.e. seeking adult help, saying "I'm sick" and giving descriptive information)

- Student will demonstrate the appropriate responses to pain (i.e. seeking adult help, saying "Ow" or "I have pain", and pointing to the area of pain)

The concept of good health is not easily understood by our students. Explaining why and how to be healthy as a part of a daily routine may help students follow through on simple, appropriate health rules.

↳ Being healthy means taking care of my body.

↳ It is important to take care of my body so that I grow strong and I don't get sick or hurt.

↳ I need to take care of my body every day.

↳ I need to eat good food every day. Mom and Dad will know what good food I need to eat. I will do a good job eating what Mom and Dad want me to eat.

↳ I need to brush my teeth every day with toothpaste, a toothbrush and water. Sometimes I may need to use dental floss.

↳ I need to take a bath or shower and wash myself with soap and water every day.

➥ I need to get plenty of sleep every night. I will go to bed when Mom or Dad tell me and sleep until it's morning and time to get up. It's important to get a good night's sleep.

➥ I need to wash my hands before I eat or make food and after I use the toilet or blow my nose.

➥ I need to do some exercise every day. Exercise will keep my body strong and healthy. I can walk, run, jump and do exercises. My teachers and parents will help me exercise.

➥ When I'm sick or have pain I must tell an adult and my parents. Adults like my teachers, nurses, neighbors, and family members can help me when I'm sick or have pain.

 I will do a good job of taking care of my body. I will do a good job of being healthy.

It's rare to find a student with autism who will eat a healthy, balanced diet consisting of various foods. Parents frequently complain to educators that they have tried everything to get their kids to eat a variety of good foods. This is an example of a story about eating healthy foods. I tell parents to read a story like this to their children as often as they can and to persistently introduce good foods to them. Start small. At school we often insist that students just lick or taste something, or swallow a miniscule bite at first. Always reward students for trying new foods, and be persistent as well as consistent with your eating routine.

Eating Fruits and Vegetables

⮱ Fruits and vegetables are good foods to eat.

⮱ Fruits and vegetables are full of vitamins and good things for my body. Everyone needs to eat fruits and vegetables. I need to eat fruits and vegetables every day.

⮱ There are many different fruits to eat. Most fruit is sweet and juicy. I could eat apples, bananas, oranges, grapes, pears, strawberries, peaches and watermelon.

⮱ I can eat raw fruit, or fruit cooked in pies. I can eat fruit in jam or jelly. I can drink fruit juice. I can eat fruit mixed with lots of things.

⮱ There are many kinds of fruit. I might not like all fruits, but I need to try lots of different fruits to decide which ones I like best.

⮱ Fruits are delicious and good for me. I need to do a good job eating fruit every day.

⮱ Vegetables are tasty and good for my body. I need to eat lots of vegetables every day.

⇨ Some vegetables are good in a salad. I can eat lettuce, tomatoes, cucumbers, carrots, celery, and lots of other vegetables in a salad.

⇨ I can eat vegetables with dip. Broccoli, carrots, celery, green peppers and cauliflower taste good with dip.

⇨ Some vegetables taste good cooked. Corn, beans, green peas, onions, asparagus, spinach and potatoes taste good cooked with butter and salt.

⇨ There are lots of ways to eat vegetables. I can taste lots of vegetables and decide which ones I like best.

⇨ There are many vegetables to eat. I might not like all the vegetables, but I will taste many vegetables to decide which ones I like best.

⇨ Fruits and vegetables are good for my body. Eating fruits and vegetables will help me be strong and healthy.

I will do a good job eating some fruits and vegetables every day.

Bedtime is a common battle for students with autism and other disabilities. Establishing a consistent time for bed as well as a bedtime routine is recommended. This story explains to students why sleep is important.

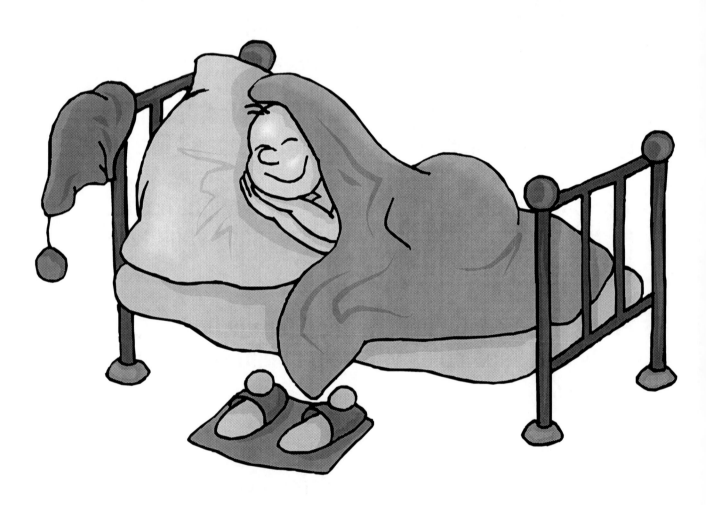

I Sleep At Night

➲ Everybody needs to sleep.

➲ Mommy and Daddy and everyone I know need to sleep.

➲ Even animals need to sleep.

➲ I need to sleep.

➲ Every night my body feels tired and I know I need to sleep.

➲ Most people sleep at night. I know I need to sleep every night at bedtime.

➲ Mommy and Daddy know when I need to go to bed and sleep.

➲ When it's time to sleep Mommy and Daddy may say, "Time for bed".

➲

➭ I will get in my bed and get ready to sleep.

➭ Maybe I'll hear a story or some music before I sleep. Maybe I will hug a stuffed animal. I know I need to lie quietly so that I can fall asleep.

➭ Mommy and Daddy know when I need to wake up. After sleeping all night I will feel awake and happy and my body will feel ready to do things.

➭ If I don't sleep all night, I will feel tired, unhappy and I won't feel ready to do things.

➭ It's important to have a good night's sleep. I know I need to stay in bed and stay asleep all night.

 My body needs to sleep every night. I will do a good job of sleeping at night.

Being able to tell someone you are sick is one of the most important things a student with disabilities needs to learn to do effectively. The following story introduces the concept of sickness. If a student doesn't understand what it means to be sick, they may not realize it can be a problem and that they need to tell a responsible adult. Being sick can be scary and sometimes dangerous. It's essential that students learn to tell others, not just their parents, when they are sick.

Sometimes I Feel Sick

⮧ Sometimes people get sick.

⮧ Mom and Dad get sick sometimes.

⮧ Teachers get sick.

⮧ My friends get sick.

⮧ Sometimes I get sick.

⮧ I might be sick with a headache.

⮧ I might have a tummy ache.

⮧ I might have a fever and feel hot and dizzy.

⮧ Sometimes, I will feel very tired and need to stay in bed.

⮧ When I feel sick I must tell an adult. I can tell Mommy, Daddy, or my teachers.

⮧ I may need to go to the school nurse. I will tell the nurse what feels sick. Adults will know what to do when I am sick.

☝ Sometimes, I might have a cold.

☝ When I cough, I need to cover my mouth.

☝ When my nose is runny, I need to use a tissue and wipe and blow my nose.

☝ When I wipe my nose and mouth, I also need to wash my hands with soap and water.

☝ When I am sick, I might need to stay home.

☝ I might need to take medicine to feel better. Mommy or Daddy will give me the medicine I need to take. I will do a good job of taking medicine.

☝ People don't like being sick. I don't like being sick. But Mom and Dad will know how to help me get better.

☝ I don't know how long I will be sick. When I feel better, I will go back to school.

Mom or Dad will decide when I feel better and can go back to school.

The following is a repeated line story that can be created using photos or line drawings. The repeated line could be read by the student, or activated using a simple, voice output device switch, such as a Big Mack, and the pictured phrase can be placed using velcro onto each page. This is an easy format to use with a variety of topics, and the repeated line helps students remember what they need to say.

I Feel Sick — A repeated line story

➪ I have a tummy ache.
   I need to say…"I feel sick."

➪ I have a sore throat.
   I need to say…"I feel sick."

➪ I have a headache.
   I need to say…"I feel sick."

➪ My head feels hot and tired.
   I need to say…"I feel sick."

➪ I have a runny nose.
   I need to say…"I feel sick."

➪ I'm coughing and coughing.
   I need to say…"I feel sick."

⤵ Sometimes I feel sick.
I need to tell Mommy or a teacher..."I feel sick."

Adults will help me feel better. Soon I won't feel sick and I can say..."I feel good!"

The Picture Communication Symbols copyright 1981-2002, Mayer-Johnson, Inc. Used with permission.

I Feel Sick (A repeated line story.) was created using the Picture It Software Program (Slater Software, Inc.) and Boardmaker pictures (Mayer-Johnson, Inc.) and the repeated line is recorded on a Big Mack switch (Ablenet, Inc)

The concept of pain, like that of sickness, is an important one for students with autism to understand. It is especially important to teach them to tell an adult when they experience it. I use the term pain instead of hurt, because pain is a word typically without multiple meanings. It specifically implies physical discomfort and injury. Because we don't use it as often, the word pain can take on an important connotation, not unlike an emergency term. We can teach students to use the word pain and point to the area of pain on their body when they tell adults. Learning about pain and telling adults when they experience it is an extremely important life-long skill.

Sometimes I Have Pain

↳ People have pain sometimes.

↳ Sometimes I might have pain.

↳ Sometimes I have pain in my head.

↳ Sometimes I have pain in my tummy.

↳ Sometimes I have pain in my arm or leg.

↳ Sometimes I have pain somewhere else on my body.

↳ Pain feels bad.

↳ Pain can make me sad.

↳ Pain can make me cry.

↳ Pain can make me upset and mad.

- I need to tell Mommy or Daddy and my teachers when I have pain.

- When I have pain, I can say, "ouch!"

- I can say, "I hurt, I have pain."

- I will show an adult where I have pain. I can point to the spot that hurts.

- Mommy and Daddy and my teachers will help me when I have pain.

- Pain hurts. Pain feels bad. I always need to tell adults when I have pain.

- Adults will help me feel better. Mommy or Daddy may need to give me medicine to make the pain go away.

 I will do a good job telling adults when I have pain. Soon pain will go away and I will feel fine again.

Doctors' appointments can be challenging for students with autism because they can't predict what will happen to them. If they've already had a bad experience at a doctor's office, they won't want to go back. The following story may help to prepare students for these types of situations. It explains why we need to go to the doctor, what might happen there and how long the visit might be. Discussing fears and feelings about seeing a doctor will help relieve anxieties.

⇨ Sometimes, people need to go to the doctor. Mommy and Daddy and other people sometimes go to the doctor.

⇨ Sometimes, I need to go to the doctor.

⇨ The doctor and the nurses help people. The doctor and the nurses want me to be healthy and feel good.

⇨ The doctor may need to check my body to make sure everything is okay. If I feel sick or have pain the doctor will check to find out what's wrong.

⇨ Going to the doctor is not always fun. I may be sad and upset about going to the doctor. But I know it's important for a doctor to check me, and help me feel better.

🖐 Mommy or Daddy will be with me when the doctor checks me. Mommy or Daddy will help me feel better.

🖐 Soon my doctor visit will be finished and I can go home.

🖐 Most people go to their doctor at least once a year. I will probably go to the doctor every year. Sometimes, I may need to go to the doctor's a lot.

🖐 It's okay to go to the doctor's office. My visit to the doctor's office probably won't take much time.

 I know I need to go to the doctor's office sometimes. The doctor wants to help me be healthy. The doctor will do a good job. I will do a good job when I go to the doctor's office.

Going to the dentist can be traumatic for anyone, but especially for someone with autism. To prepare your child for a dental appointment, remind him/her that dentists touch people's teeth and this is okay. Emphasize appropriate behavior, such as sitting still, and that soon the visit to the dentist will be over. The following is a simple, generic story about going to the dentist. You may need to create more specific, personalized stories about the experience.

Going to the Dentist

⇨ People need to go to the dentist. Dentists help our teeth stay healthy and clean.

⇨ Mom and Dad and everyone go to the dentist. I will go to the dentist too.

⇨ The dentist will look at my teeth and touch my teeth. Sometimes the dentist will put something in my mouth when he checks my teeth. The dentist wants to be sure my teeth are healthy.

⇨ Sometimes, a dental hygienist will clean my teeth with a special toothbrush and toothpaste. The dental hygienist will make my teeth very clean and healthy.

⇨ Sometimes, the dentist will find something wrong with my teeth. Maybe I will have a cavity.

⇨ A cavity is a bad thing for my teeth. The dentist will work hard to get rid of the cavity. I need to do a good job and sit still so the dentist can fix the cavity.

🖎 It is not always fun going to the dentist. Maybe I will feel scared and upset when the dentist touches my teeth.

🖎 I can tell Mom and Dad and the dentist that I'm scared. They will help me feel better.

🖎 I know that sometimes I need to go to the dentist. The dentist will need to touch and look at my teeth. The dentist wants to help my teeth be strong and healthy.

🖎 I will do a good job at the dentist. I will sit still and let the dentist touch my teeth. I will remember to tell the dentist when I'm scared and upset.

🖎 My dentist visit will be finished soon, and then I can leave. The dentist does a good job helping my teeth. I do a good job at the dentist!

I do a good job at the dentist!

As with many changes, students with autism may have a hard time dealing with bandages. They may not like the look or feel of a bandage and try to take it off. It helps to explain why the bandage is there and how long it needs to stay on.

Wearing A Bandage

➪ Sometimes if I get hurt, I will need to wear a bandage.

➪ When I get a cut or a scrape that bleeds, I may need to wear a bandage.

➪ I may need to wear a bandage on my finger, my arm, my leg, my head or some other part of my body. A bandage will help make my hurt or cut get better.

➪ Some bandages are big, for big cuts, and some bandages are small, for small cuts. Bandages will keep my cuts clean and stop the bleeding.

➪ My mom, a teacher or a nurse may decide that I need a bandage for a cut or scrap.

↬ I might not like a bandage. A bandage may feel strange and uncomfortable. But I know that a bandage will help my cut get better, and stop the bleeding.

↬ When Mom or another adult puts on a bandage to help a cut, I need to keep the bandage on.

↬ The bandage needs to stay on my cut to keep it clean and help my cut get better. When my cut is all better, the bandage can come off. Mom will know when to take the bandage off.

↬ Sometimes when I get hurt I will need to wear a bandage. I might not like the bandage, but I know the bandage will help my hurt get better.

 **I will do a good job of keeping bandages on my cuts and hurts.**

There are several reasons for teaching students not to touch blood. Cuts and open wounds are susceptible to infections. With dirt and germs easily transmitted by hands, it's important to teach students not to touch their own cuts and scrapes. All bodily fluids can carry diseases, but especially blood. Students need to know it's not okay to touch blood, but especially someone else's blood.

I Don't Touch Blood

↳ I don't touch blood.

↳ Blood is dirty and yucky. Sometimes Blood can be full of germs.

↳ When I have a cut or scrape and there is blood, I must be careful not to touch it.

↳ I don't want to get dirt or germs on my cut and I don't want my blood to get on people or things.

↳ When I have a cut or scrape I need to tell an adult. I should tell Mom or Dad, a teacher or a nurse, when I have a cut.

↳ An adult will wash off the blood and clean my cut. An adult will know how to take care of a cut.

⮎ Sometimes other people have cuts and bleed. It's never okay to touch someone else's blood.

⮎ If my friend or a classmate, or anyone has blood, I must never touch it.

⮎ Blood is dirty and yucky. Blood can have germs. I never touch blood.

⮎ If blood gets on my hands or any part of me, I must wash carefully with soap and water.

⮎ I will remember not to touch blood.

⮎ If I have blood from a cut I won't touch it. I will tell an adult and the adult will clean my blood off.

⮎ I won't touch blood on anyone. Blood is dirty and can make me sick.

 If blood gets on my hands or any part of me I will do a good job washing it off with soap and water.

Many students with disabilities, including autism, take medication. Although most students eventually get used to taking medication, some need some convincing. I believe it's important to explain to students the reasons we take medicine as well as the dangers of taking the wrong medicine or taking medicine without appropriate supervision.

Taking Medicine

↳ Sometimes, I may need to take medicine.

↳ Everybody takes medicine sometimes.

↳ Mommy and Daddy and everyone I know needs to take medicine sometimes.

↳ Medicine can help people.

↳ There are all kinds of medicine. Some medicines help when you are sick. Some medicines help for pain.

↳ Medicines help people do a better job. I may need to take medicine to help me feel better and do a good job.

↳ If Mommy or Daddy or a nurse tell me to take medicine, I know I need to take it and swallow it because the medicine will help me.

↳

🖐 But not all medicines are right for me. The wrong medicines can make me feel bad and sick. I only take medicines that Mom, Dad, a nurse or teacher give me.

🖐 I must never take medicine from students, friends or other adults. I must never take medicine from someone I don't know.

🖐 I will do a good job of taking my medicine. I know that my medicine will help me. I also know I can't take medicine by myself and I must never take someone else's medicine.

 I will do a good job of taking my medicine.

Creating Question-Answer Health Cards

The following questions and answers can be created on large cards, front and back. Visual cues, such as pictures, are recommended with all questions and answers. This activity can be used with a group of students, one-on-one with an adult, or independently, for self-checking.

Health Question-Answer Cards:

1. What can I eat that's good for me?

Answers: fruit, vegetables, meat or fish, dairy, nuts and bread
(Note: These answers may vary according to individual students' dietary needs.)

2. Why do we need to drink plenty of water and other beverages?

Answers: to help us get well, for healthy skin and hair, and to keep our body healthy.

3. Why do we need plenty of sleep?

Answers: to think better, to do a good job at our work, to keep us from getting sick, and to keep us strong and healthy.

4. Why do we need exercise?

Answers: to be strong, to help us grow, to feel healthy, and to become athletes.

5. Who can get sick?

Answer: Everybody: kids, adults, mom, dad, grandparents, me.

6. What can we be sick with?

Answers: stomach aches, sore throats, colds or coughs, diarrhea, vomiting, fever and flu.

7. How does it feel to be sick?

Answer: feels bad, it feels yucky, it can be painful; it makes you tired, it makes you sad

8. What should I do when I'm sick?

Answers: tell someone, tell mom or dad, tell my teachers, wash my hands, rest in bed, do what mom tells me.

9. Who can have pain?

Answer: Everybody: kids, adults, mom, dad, grandparents, me.

10. What can cause pain?

Answers: cuts, bruises, toothaches, tummy aches, sore throats, headaches, something hurting inside my body.

11. What should I do when I have pain?

Answers: tell mom and dad, tell teachers, tell a nurse; ask adults to help me.

12. Why do we need to wear bandages?

Answers: to keep cuts clean, to protect cuts, to stop bleeding, to help cuts heal and get better.

MODESTY

- Being Naked
- Where Can I Be Naked
- My Clothes Need to Stay On
- Dressing Myself
- My Private Areas
- No Hands Down My Pants
- People Need Privacy

Modesty is the foundation for safe and acceptable personal behavior in social situations

Teaching Modesty

Modesty becomes an important issue as students grow older and their bodies begin to mature. Some individuals may not realize they are growing and changing, and their bodies will look and feel different. Likewise they may not understand the significance of their body changes and why they need to be clothed. As students with disabilities begin adolescence, they may have difficulty adjusting to the new rules which dictate modesty.

The concept of modesty should be introduced early, usually when children are able to dress and undress independently. People tend to be more tolerant of very young children (five and under) taking off their clothes in public. But as children become older, it is no longer "cute," or will be tolerated. Parents may mistakenly believe that a child will naturally become more modest as he or she gets older. This may be true of typically-developing children, but is often not the case with students with disabilities. If we wait to begin teaching modesty to students with autism until they are older or when we find their behavior has become problematic, it may be a very difficult issue to address.

I once worked with a family whose autistic daughter liked to undress when she was home. She habitually did this from the time she was very young, often stripping naked if she felt hot or uncomfortable. The parents allowed this behavior, thinking she would eventually outgrow it. By the age of 12, she had entered puberty and her body was developing predictably. The parents tried to change this behavior when they realized she was an adolescent and wasn't going to stop on her own. But they met with no success. When she appeared naked at a neighborhood block party, they also realized that her immodest habit had now become an embarrassing problem which could even threaten their daughter's personal safety.

When teaching modesty, it's important to teach students what being naked means and why it's okay to expose some parts of their body but not other parts. This is when you need to discuss private areas, such as genitals, and that it's not okay for others to see you naked and it's not okay to expose private areas. It's especially important to discuss where and in what circumstances a person can be naked. A simple rule to teach most students is: you can be naked in your bedroom or bathroom, if you are alone with the door shut. Obviously this rule would not necessarily apply to students who need help dressing and bathing. But for those students who are physically capable of dressing and bathing themselves, it is essential that they learn to do it independently, to the best of their ability, before beginning puberty. This will help them to understand and practice modesty before their growing and changing bodies make it an absolute necessity.

Students should learn that people's clothes need to stay on and that it is socially inappropriate to expose our underwear, lift our shirts or skirts, and pull down our pants in public. The same rule applies: we only take off our clothes in designated areas, like locker rooms, our bedrooms or bathrooms.

Although we teach students that they should not be naked or expose private areas to others, there are obvious exceptions to this rule, such as when a doctor or parent/caregiver may occasionally need to see the child naked for purposes of examining, or for assistance with hygiene and dressing. Parents and teachers should discuss these possible exceptions to the rule, but should also emphasize when it's never okay for someone to see you naked. For example, I tell students it is never okay for strangers, other students, neighbors, and adults other than doctors, nurses, parents or trusted caregivers to see them naked.

It is also essential to teach what a person should do when someone asks to see them naked, takes off their clothes or asks to see private areas, such as their genitals, bottom or breasts. Students need to understand that it is a violation of their personal safety. Always teach them to say "No", and to tell parents or trusted adults whenever anyone violates their modesty, regardless of who that might be. It is better to have this telling response be over-learned, rather than not learned at all. For example, if your child tells you that grandma or the doctor saw him naked, praise him for telling you, even though it may not be a problem situation. Children should get in the practice of habitually telling parents when anyone sees them naked or, in any way, violates their personal safety.

Obeying certain rules of modesty is important in our culture. Exposing oneself in public is an illegal, and at times, immoral action. The consequences of immodesty can be dangerous as well as embarrassing. Immodesty threatens an individual's personal safety. Not only does it cause others to be shocked and angered, but it can also invite molestation and sexual abuse.

The goals and anticipated progression of skills for this unit:

- The student will demonstrate understanding of naked and differentiate between naked and clothed figures.

- The student will identify appropriate places to be naked.

- The student will identify which areas of his/her body should be covered.

- The student will identify appropriate ways to wear clothing.

- The student will demonstrate who can and who cannot see him/her naked.

- The student will demonstrate how to tell a trusted adult when someone asks to see them naked or causes them to be naked or undressed.

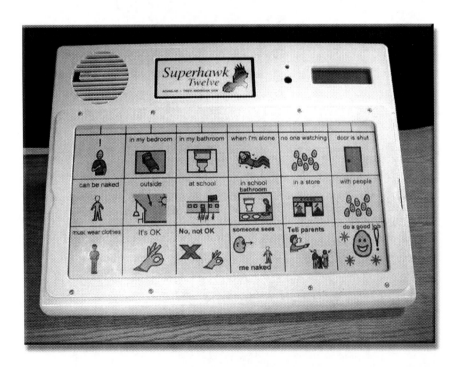

Voice output devices such as the Superhawk (Adamlab-MB) allow students to respond verbally to questions and information presented.

In order to teach the concept of modesty we need to talk about the concept of naked versus wearing clothes, and establish rules for where nudity is and isn't socially acceptable. This story focuses on private areas and the importance of keeping private areas covered. You will notice that I underline the word 'not'. This is a term many of our students don't understand. You will want to emphasize this word or replace it with 'no' or another negative word your students use in order to insure comprehension.

Being Naked

↳ Being naked means wearing no clothes.

↳ Sometimes, it's okay for people to see a naked baby.

↳ It is <u>not</u> okay for people to see you or me naked.

↳ Sometimes it is okay for a doctor or a nurse and my mom to see me naked.

↳ It is <u>not</u> okay for students, friends or other adults to see me naked.

↳ It is <u>not</u> okay for people to show their naked private areas.

↳ If someone tries to see my private areas, I need to say, "No!"

- If someone tries to see my private areas, I need to tell a teacher and my parents.

- I need to be naked when I take a bath or shower and when I change my clothes.

- It is okay to be naked if I am alone in my bedroom and the door is shut.

- It is okay to be naked if I am alone in my bathroom at home and the door is shut.

- It is <u>not</u> okay to be naked at school.

- It is <u>not</u> okay to be naked outside.

- It is <u>not</u> okay to be naked in most places.

- Sometimes it is okay to change clothes and be naked in another bathroom. But I need to be alone and the door needs to be shut.

➥ It is <u>not</u> okay for people to see me naked and it's <u>not</u> okay for me to see other people naked.

➥ If someone tries to see me naked, I will tell them "No," and tell a teacher and a parent.

➥ I am <u>not</u> a baby. It is <u>not</u> okay for people to see me naked.

 I will do a good job and remember to be alone in my bedroom or my bathroom with the door shut when I am naked.

Activities to determine student comprehension of the concept of modesty

It's important to create activities which allow students to indicate to parents and teachers that they know where they can and cannot be naked. In order to do this, you should first take pictures of actual familiar places, including the student's bedroom, bathroom, other rooms in his/her home, outside places, stores, school areas, and even unfamiliar places. If the student is higher functioning, you might use more abstract pictures to represent these places. Enlarge these pictures and laminate them. Take a picture of the student clothed and use a line drawing picture of a person naked. (It is not appropriate to use photos of a student naked.) Using these pictures, you can ask the student to decide if he/she can be naked or should be clothed in the various pictured places. The student can place an appropriate picture of himself/herself in these pictures either clothed or naked. It may be helpful to attach Velcro to each place picture and to each person picture. I use Velcro a lot to help students independently respond in a given activity. The Velcro acts as a prompt for the student to attach the answer. This is a good way to check for comprehension of this concept. This is also a good activity to use with students who are non-verbal or have limited verbal language, but can demonstrate the appropriate answers using visual-tactile responses.

People occasionally ask why I teach students not to be naked in other rooms in their home such as the kitchen or living room. Although each home has different rules, if an individual is used to being naked in various rooms in his home, this may become a problem if, for example, guests are visiting, maintenance personnel (plumbers, etc.) are working in the house, or unexpected visitors arrive.

Where Can I Be Naked?

NO

Outside
At school
In stores
In my kitchen
In my living room
In my yard
In other people's houses
In other bedrooms

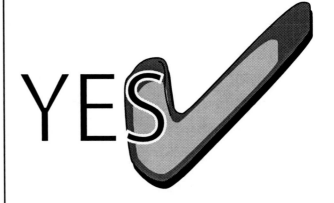

YES

In my bedroom
In my bathroom
Doctor's office

It may be necessary to use actual photos of places to teach the modesty concept.

Wearing clothes appropriately and not disrobing or exposing certain areas of our body in public are key elements to the rules of modesty. But, it can be a hard concept to teach because of the subtleties involved. For example, although it's okay to take off a cardigan sweater or outer garment in public, it's not okay to remove pants or lift up shirts in public. And while in some public places it's okay to remove shoes and socks, that's not always appropriate at school or restaurants. The following story talks about the need to keep clothes on and to not expose underwear or do inappropriate things with our clothing in public (i.e: pulling down pants, lifting shirts, etc.). Depending upon the needs of an individual student, you may want to compose a story that addresses specific, immodest behaviors.

My Clothes Need To Stay On

↳ People wear clothes every day.

↳ We wear lots of clothes when we're cold and when it's winter.

↳ We wear only a few clothes when we're hot and when it's summer.

↳ We always wear clothes that cover our private areas.

↳ We wear clothes everywhere. We wear clothes at school, at home, outside, in a car, on a bus, when it's hot and when it's cold. We wear clothes everywhere.

↳ Our clothes need to stay on. I need to wear my clothes every day. I can only take off my clothes in my bedroom or a bathroom with the door shut.

➪ People should not see me take off my clothes. People should not see my underwear. People should never see me naked.

➪ My clothes need to stay on. I don't lift my shirt or pull down my pants in front of people.

 I know I need to wear clothes everyday. I will do a good job of keeping my clothes on.

The Picture Communication Symbols copyright 1981-2002, Mayer-Johnson, Inc. Used with permission.

A Big Mack single voice output switch can allow non-verbal or limitedly verbal students to respond while reading the story.

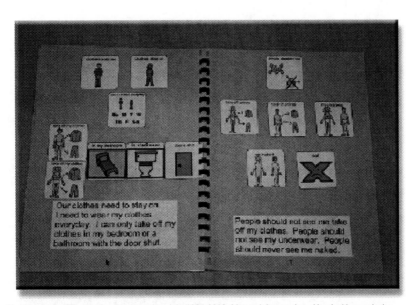

The Picture Communication Symbols copyright 1981-2002, Mayer-Johnson, Inc. Used with permission.

The story pages can be illustrated using one picture or several pictures as shown. It is helpful to point to the pictures as you or the student read the story.

When we teach students about modesty, we obviously need to teach them to dress and undress themselves. If a student isn't managing his own dressing routine, he can not be expected to consistently demonstrate modesty. The following story can prepare a student to learn this skill and also provides a step-by-step guide to appropriate self-dressing.

Dressing Myself

☞ I can dress myself.

☞ Most people get dressed by themselves. Adults, Mom and Dad, big boys and big girls all dress themselves. I can dress myself too.

☞ When I was little and didn't know how to dress myself, Mom or Dad would help me get dressed.

☞ Now I'm a big boy(girl) and I can get dressed by myself.

☞ I might worry about getting dressed by myself. Maybe it will be hard or I won't get my clothes on right.

☞ I need to practice getting my clothes on and soon I will do it right.

☞

☝ I can get dressed slowly and carefully so I can do a good job. If I have a problem getting dressed, I can always ask Mom or Dad for a little help.

☝ I know I will do a good job of getting dressed by myself.

1. I take off all of my dirty clothes or pajamas before I put on my clean clothes.

2. I put on clean underwear first. I put on underpants, and sometimes an undershirt (or bra). I look to make sure the labels are inside my underpants and I put them on right.

3. I put on clean pants and a clean shirt. I make sure my clothes are not inside out. The labels should be inside the clothes.

4. I zip up my pants, if I have a zipper. I button all my buttons on my shirt and pants. When I look down, I should see the front of my clothes.

5. I put on a pair of socks (one sock on each foot) I will make sure my socks match or look alike. If my socks feel funny, maybe I put them on wrong and need to fix them.

6. I put on my shoes. I make sure my shoes match, and they are on the right foot. Sometimes, if my feet feel funny, it's because my shoes are on the wrong feet. I can switch my shoes if they are on the wrong feet.

7. If my shoes have laces, I may need help tying them. I will try to tie my shoes first before I ask someone to help me.

 Now I'm dressed! I did a good job of dressing myself. I am a big boy(girl) and I can dress myself. I will dress myself again tomorrow.

It is okay to teach private areas to students as young as five years if circumstances warrant it. I recommend it if they are demonstrating problematic behavior such as exposure in public, and if they are able to understand the concept of private areas. It may be necessary to modify this story if you are using it with a younger student. Discussing the topic of private areas occasionally encourages students to take an increased interest in them and they may demonstrate some of the immodest behaviors we wanted to avoid.

My Private Areas

☞ Everyone has private areas on their body. Mom and Dad have private areas. All adults and children have private areas. I have private areas.

☞ Our private areas are covered by underwear or swimsuits.

☞ My underwear and swimsuit cover my private areas.

☞ Private areas can have many names. My breasts, bottom and genitals are my private areas. I might use other names for my private areas.

☞ My private areas belong to me. People should <u>not</u> see or touch my private areas. Most of the time, my private areas need to be covered with clothing.

➦ Sometimes my mom or dad, a doctor or a nurse may need to see my private areas. Most of the time, I'm the only one to see my private areas.

➦ I need to keep my private areas covered.

➦ Usually the only times my private areas are uncovered and naked are when I'm using the toilet, taking a bath or shower, or getting dressed.

 My private areas belong to me. I will do a good job of keeping my private areas covered.

It's not uncommon for children to put their hands down their pants. They may need to scratch themselves or adjust their underwear. Sometimes putting hands down their pants is a comfort or calming response. Regardless of why a student is putting his or her hands down thier pants, there are social and hygiene rules that need to be followed. Students need to be taught that this is a private behavior and that it's also unhygienic. You might not be able to eliminate this behavior, especially if a student has been exhibiting it for a long time. But establishing and adhering to appropriate rules, will help to manage this behavior.

No Hands Down My Pants

↳ It's usually <u>not</u> okay to put my hands down my pants.

↳ Sometimes I may want to put my hands down my pants.

↳ Sometimes I need to scratch my bottom or fix my underwear.

↳ Putting my hands down my pants is private. I will remember to be alone if I put my hands down my pants.

↳ I can only put my hands down my pants when I'm alone in my bedroom or bathroom with the door shut.

↳ It's <u>not</u> okay to put my hands down my pants at school.

↳ It's <u>not</u> okay to put my hands down my pants when any kids or adults are watching.

↳ People should never see me putting my hands down my pants.

↳ If I need to scratch my bottom or fix my underwear, I will be alone in my bedroom or bathroom with the door shut.

↳ My hands get dirty and stinky when I put them down my pants.

↳ I must wash my hands with soap and water if I put them down my pants.

↳ Every time I put my hands down my pants I must wash my hands with soap and water.

↳ Sometimes I might need to put my hands down my pants.

↳ I will remember to be alone in my bedroom or a bathroom when I put my hands down my pants.

↳ People won't see me put my hands down my pants. I will be private.

 I will remember to wash my hands every time I put my hands down my pants.

Sometimes students are curious about other people when they change clothes, shower or use the toilet. They may attempt to watch others when people are trying to demonstrate modesty. It is important to teach students that everyone needs privacy sometimes, and that it is rude and inappropriate to stare at others when they need their privacy. It is also very inappropriate for students to witness sexual acts. Students should learn that knocking on doors and apologizing and turning away are appropriate responses to intruding on others' privacy.

People Need Privacy

↳ Everyone changes clothes. Everyone is naked sometimes. Everyone uses the toilet and takes a bath or shower.

↳ People want privacy when they take off their clothes and use the bathroom. It is <u>not</u> okay to watch other people take off their clothes. It is <u>not</u> okay to try to see people naked.

↳ It is <u>not</u> okay for people to see me naked and, it's <u>not</u> okay for me to see other people naked.

↳ When someone is trying to change their clothes and needs privacy, I will remember not to stare. I will look away and not peek at people when they change clothes, take a bath or shower and use the toilet.

↳ I don't want people to watch me when I do private things and I won't watch other people doing private things.

☝ People need privacy when they change clothes, take a bath or shower, and use the toilet. It is <u>not</u> okay to watch people when they are doing private things.

☝ I need to knock on bathroom doors when I think someone is using the toilet or taking a bath. I need to knock on bedroom doors when someone is changing clothes or in bed.

☝ It is rude and wrong to watch people when they need privacy in a bedroom or bathroom.

☝ If I see someone doing something private like changing, taking a shower, using the toilet, or in bed, I will say, "Excuse me," "I'm sorry," and I will leave that person alone.

 I will do a good job of respecting other people's privacy.

GROWTH AND DEVELOPMENT

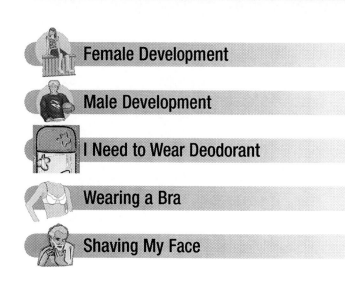

Female Development

Male Development

I Need to Wear Deodorant

Wearing a Bra

Shaving My Face

Preparing students for the body changes of puberty will minimize fear and confusion

Teaching Growth and Development

People with autism typically dislike change. They usually like predictability and routine. For this reason, I've often had students with autism who refuse to "get older." One student had a hard time accepting that every year on his birthday he was a new year older. Other students have had a hard time understanding and accepting the concept of getting bigger and outgrowing their clothes.

Growth and development can be a difficult concept to understand, especially if you are growing and changing so slowly that you can't perceive many of the changes in your physical appearance. Even though puberty is a slow process, the physical changes are dramatic.

Boys, often at about the age of 12, begin to grow pubic hair, and thicker hair on their legs. They begin to sweat more and excrete body odors. They may have a growth spurt; their feet and noses may get bigger. As they grow older, their chests get broader, their muscles become more defined and their voices get deeper. Underarm hair and facial hair begin to grow at about the age of 15. They develop an Adam's apple. The boys continue to grow and develop until they are about 20 years old.

Girls often start puberty at younger ages than boys. The first signs of puberty are the beginning growth of the breasts and the appearance of pubic hair, and these changes may occur in girls as young as eight. Girls will often have pubic hair by the time they are 10 or 11, and most will have their first period between the ages of 11 and 12. Typically, they continue to grow in height, weight and breast size until they are about 16. A good rule of thumb for determining the onset of menstruation; a girl may have her first menstrual period approximately one year to two years after pubic hair begins to grow. However, girls grow and mature at different rates, so it's not easy to determine exactly when menstruation will occur. It may be helpful for parents to discuss these changes with their child's doctor or a school nurse in order to get more specific guidelines for determining when menstruation will begin.

I've found it's important to prepare students for the changes to their body before they actually begin puberty. This is especially true for students with autism.

I had one student several years ago who typically disliked change of any kind, but especially had trouble with any change to himself. This student, who I'll call Clark, was independent with his hygiene skills and learned to be appropriately modest as he grew older. When he started to grow pubic hair at the age of 12, his mother discovered how much it upset him after he attempted to shave it off using his sister's razor. In his mother's words, it was a "bloodbath." Clark didn't understand why hair was growing near his genitals, and he decided to get rid of it the only way he knew how. After we explained to him that pubic hair was all part of growing up and that it was supposed to be there, he learned to accept that change as a natural progression to getting older.

The goal with this unit is not only to prepare students for the changes that will occur as they grow and develop, but also to help them accept the fact that this is okay. Their bodies will continue to grow and change as they start to look like young adults and eventually reach their adult heights. The following stories, some of which are gender specific, will help prepare students for the inevitable growth changes that will occur and help them learn new hygiene routines to add to their daily schedule. As with all units that teach skills related to puberty, it is recommended that students be segregated and taught information pertaining to their own gender.

The goals and anticipated progression of skills for this unit:

- Student will identify basic body changes of puberty: increased height and weight, hair growth, breast development, penis growth, body odor, etc.

- Student will understand the term deodorant and demonstrate its use.

- Student will independently apply deodorant as a part of his daily hygiene routine.

- Female student will tolerate wearing a bra.

- Female student will independently put on a bra as a part of her daily dressing routine.

The Picture Communication Symbols copyright 1981-2002, Mayer-Johnson, Inc. Used with permission.

The following two stories are gender specific and designed to help students understand and accept the changes to their bodies as they grow and mature. All of these changes can be scary to students. The more we prepare them for these changes and assure them that they will be okay, the easier this transition will become.

Female Development

Our Bodies Are Growing And Changing

↳ Our bodies are growing.

↳ Every year, our bodies grow and change a little or a lot.

↳ Sometimes, we grow taller.

↳ Sometimes, we grow heavier.

↳ Soon our bodies will change in other ways.

↳ I will start to grow hair on my body.

↳ I will grow some hair under my arms and on my privates.

↳ I will begin to grow breasts. I will need to wear a bra.

↳ Soon, I will start my period.

↳ Blood will come from my privates (out of my vagina). Blood will come out every month for about five days and then stop. This is called my "period."

↳ During my period, I will need to wear pads in my panties to catch the blood. My body is starting to grow into a woman's body.

↳ I will start to grow to look like Mommy and other adult women.

↳ I will grow and change every year until I am about 15 years old.

↳ I know that my body is growing and changing.

↳ I know that someday I will look like Mommy and other adult women.

↳ I know that soon I will get my period and blood will come out between my legs from my vagina. I know this is okay.

I will do a good job of growing and changing. It's okay to grow and change and become a woman.

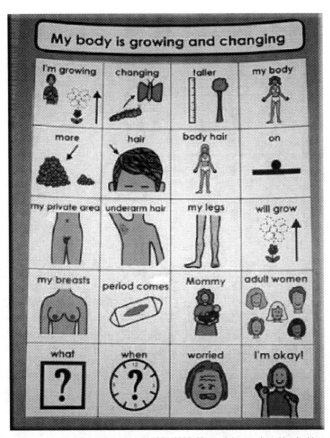

The Picture Communication Symbols copyright 1981-2002, Mayer-Johnson, Inc. Used with permission.

Communication boards help students to understand and respond to information more easily. Since many of our students are visually strong and need visual cues to help them express themselves, it is important to use these communication supplements when we discuss topics and ask them questions.

The following story helps to explain male growth and development. As with all stories, pictures are an essential tool for showing the changes that will occur. I also encourage fathers to point out to their sons what these changes will look like by indicating their own chest, face and leg hair, underarm hair, muscles and Adam's apple. Although fathers should talk about pubic hair with their sons, I don't recommend showing pubic hair, since it's important to demonstrate rules of modesty and personal safety even within one's family.

Male Development

Our Bodies Are Growing And Changing

↳ Our bodies are growing.

↳ Every year our bodies grow and change a little or a lot.

↳ Sometimes, we grow taller.

↳ Sometimes, we grow heavier.

↳ Soon our bodies will change in other ways.

↳ I will start to grow hair on my body.

↳ I will grow hair under my arms, in my armpits, and on my privates.

↳ My chest will grow bigger and broader. I will have muscular arms.

↳ My privates will change too. My penis and testicles will get bigger.

↳

🐾 My voice will sound deeper and lower like a man's voice.

🐾 I will have an Adam's apple on my neck, just like Daddy and other men.

🐾 When I am about 15 years old, I may start to grow hair on my face. I may need to shave the hair on my face.

🐾 My body will start to grow to be a man's body.

🐾 I will start to grow to look like Daddy and other adult men.

🐾 I will grow and change every year until I am about 20 years old.

🐾 I know that my body is growing and changing.

🐾 I know that someday I will look like Daddy and other adult men. I know that all boys grow and change and that's okay.

 I will do a good job of accepting all the changes to my body. I will do a good job of taking care of my body.

It's okay to grow and change and become a man.

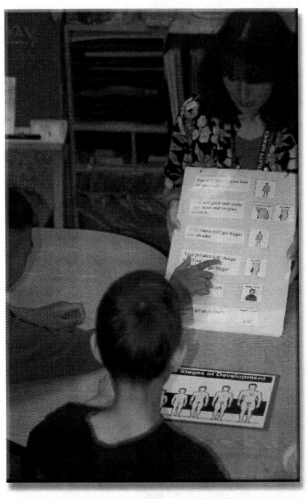

Using a variety of visual supports, as well as voice output devices help students understand information and make responses. The Cheaptalk-8 voice output device (Enabling Devices) is shown.

The Picture Communication Symbols copyright 1981-2002, Mayer-Johnson, Inc. Used with permission.

Learning to wear deodorant is another essential hygiene routine as our students get older. Most students with disabilities are not aware of the need to wear deodorant and may even resist doing so because of the change in routine, the wet feeling or the unusual smell. Parents often ask me when they should start this routine with their child. As with most changes, I tell them to start the routine of wearing deodorant before it becomes a necessity. If a student has a hard time learning or accepting new routines, it's always a good idea to start early and take it slowly. Eventually we want our students to learn to routinely put on deodorant every morning by themselves.

I Need To Wear Deodorant

↳ I'm growing older and bigger. My body is changing. Hair is starting to grow under my arms.

↳ Sometimes, my underarms will sweat and feel wet. Sometimes, my underarms will smell bad.

↳ It is important to take a shower or bath every day.

↳ I need to remember to wash my underarms with soap and water.

↳ After I take a bath or shower, I will dry my underarms with a towel. Then, I will put deodorant under my arms in a place called my armpits.

➥ The deodorant will help my underarms smell nice and stay dry. The deodorant might feel cold and wet under my arms, but soon it will dry and I will feel fine.

➥ Mom and Dad, adults and big kids wear deodorant. My body is growing big and I need to wear deodorant too.

➥ I will put on deodorant every day before I get dressed. I will smell nice and my underarms will stay dry.

 I will do a good job of wearing deodorant under my arms. I will put on deodorant every day before I get dressed.

Preparing girls for wearing bras, as with most changes, may take time. You will want to start this routine before it becomes an absolute necessity. Make sure your student demonstrates modesty and knows not to lift up her shirt or take off her clothes in public, as it is inappropriate to show people her bra. It's also important that the girls learn to put on their bras independently. The biggest problem I've faced was getting girls to remember to wear their bras every day. We used to do a discreet "bra check," to help the girls remember to check for themselves. In a room full of females, I would ask, "Who is wearing their bra today?" All the adults would discreetly pull up a bit of bra strap on their shoulder and say, "I'm wearing my bra." The students would also show a bit of strap. One non-verbal student who rarely put on her bra would usually search for her strap and find none. I would remind her to put it on the next day. Eventually, she caught on and was happy to show her bit of bra strap and be a part of our little bra-wearing club.

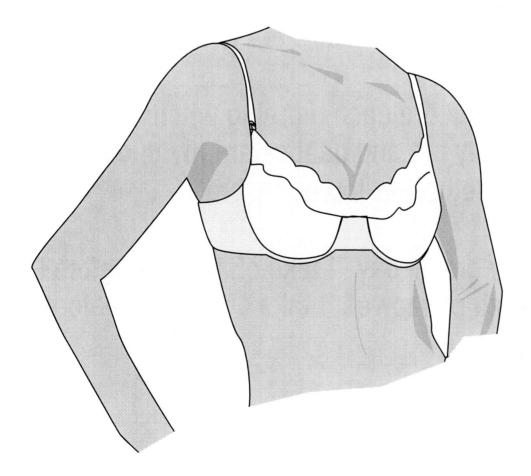

Wearing A Bra

↳ My body is growing and changing. I am starting to grow breasts. All big girls and women have breasts. Soon, I will have breasts too.

↳ Women and big girls wear bras to hold and cover their breasts. I need to wear a bra too.

↳ A bra will hold and cover my breasts. A bra will help my breasts feel comfortable. Now that I'm a big girl, I need to wear a bra every day.

↳ I will put on a bra each morning when I get dressed. My bra and panties are my underwear. I wear my clothes on top of my bra.

↳ I wear my bra all day. I take off my bra before I take a bath or shower. I take off my bra before I go to bed.

⇨ I don't need to wear a bra with my pajamas. I don't need to wear a bra when I wear a swimsuit.

⇨ I should put on a clean bra when I get dressed in the morning.

⇨ My bra and panties cover my private areas. People should <u>not</u> see me wearing my bra and panties.

⇨ Sometimes, my bra may feel uncomfortable. I can tell Mommy if my bra is too small or uncomfortable. It's important to wear a bra that feels comfortable.

⇨ I'm a big girl now. I need to wear a bra every day just like Mommy and other big girls.

I will wear a clean, comfortable bra every day. I will do a good job of wearing a bra.

Shaving is a big step for young men. Although many of them will use an electric shaver, some students may need to learn to use the potentially dangerous razor blade. I wrote this story for those daring enough to try to teach razor-type shaving. Regardless of how a student will learn to shave, it is always a good idea to teach students to shave with the help of an adult, at least until the student demonstrates safe, competent shaving skills.

Shaving My Face

➧ I'm a big boy now. My body is like a man's.

➧ Hair grows on my face just like other men. When hair on my face grows long, it is called a beard.

➧ I may need to shave off the hair on my face.

➧ Most men use a sharp razor and shaving cream to shave their faces. Some men use an electric shaver to shave their faces.

➧ Mommy or Daddy or another adult needs to help me shave my face.

➧ I should never shave unless an adult can help me.

➧ Shaving with a razor can be dangerous. I might accidentally cut my skin with the razor when I shave.

➧

☝ I need to do a careful job of shaving my face with a razor.

☝ First, I need to put shaving cream on my face.

☝ The shaving cream is like soap. It will feel cool and creamy.

☝ When the shaving cream is on my face I am ready to shave off my face hair.

☝ A razor is very sharp. I must not touch the sharp blade.

☝ I will carefully and slowly bring the razor blade down my face. I don't press the sharp razor into my skin. The razor needs to go down my face softly.

☝ The razor will take off the shaving cream and my face hair.

⮎ I must only shave off the hair under the shaving cream. I don't shave my eyebrows, nose, mouth, ears, or my eyes.

⮎ An adult must help me shave my face.

⮎ When I am finished shaving my face, I will wash off the rest of the shaving cream and then dry my face.

⮎ My face will feel smooth and soft.

⮎ If I get a small cut on my face, I will tell an adult and dab the blood with a tissue until it stops bleeding. Sometimes, men cut themselves a little when they shave.

 I will always remember to have an adult help me shave. I will remember that the razor is sharp and can cut my skin. I will do a good job of shaving carefully.

My Body is Growing and Changing
Male Development Worksheet

The following is an example of a worksheet (with the answers shown) intended for male students to fill in the appropriate answers or cut and glue pictures into the spaces provided.

1. I am growing (taller) and (heavier).

2. Hair will soon grow on my (legs, underarms,chest) and on my (privates).

3. As I get older my voice will get (lower/deeper).

4. When I am about 15, hair may start to grow on my (face).

5. I will continue to grow until I'm about (20 years old).

6. I will grow to look like my (Dad) and other (men).

7. I know I will grow and change as I get older. I feel (happy, excited, worried or okay) about growing and changing.

My Body is Growing and Changing
Female Development Worksheet

Using worksheets helps to reinforce the concepts taught and encourage problem solving and independent thinking. The following is an example of a worksheet (with the answers shown) intended for female students to fill in the appropriate answers or cut and glue pictures into the spaces provided.

1. I am growing (taller) and (heavier).

2. Hair will soon grow on my (legs, underarms) and on my (privates).

3. Soon, (breasts) will grow on my chest and I will need to wear a bra.

4. Soon, I will start to have my (period) and blood will come from between my legs.

5. When I have my period, I will need to wear (pads) in my underpants.

6. I will grow to look like my (mom) and other (women).

7. I know I will grow and change as I get older. I feel (happy, excited, worried or okay) about growing and changing.

MENSTRUATION

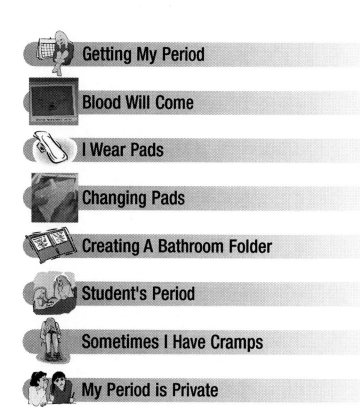

- Getting My Period
- Blood Will Come
- I Wear Pads
- Changing Pads
- Creating A Bathroom Folder
- Student's Period
- Sometimes I Have Cramps
- My Period is Private

Independent menstrual
hygiene improves quality
of life and promotes social
acceptance

Teaching Menstruation

Puberty is a confusing and sometimes frightening time for all girls. This is especially true for girls with disabilities or learning differences. Most typically developed girls can understand and accept the changes that will take place with their bodies as they begin puberty, but girls with special needs often don't understand why their bodies are changing, or that these changes are normal and appropriate.

Menstruation is an especially difficult concept to teach girls with autism because it involves not only drastic changes to their bodies, but a requirement of learning new skills to handle the necessary hygiene routines independently.

The goal of this curriculum, as with all the units in this book, is to reduce fear and distress, teach self-care skills and encourage responsibility and independence. Learning self-care of one's menstruation also allows a student to demonstrate modesty.

Several years ago, a parent approached our school nurse with concern about the onset of her daughter's period. Her daughter had autism, and although she could handle most hygiene skills on her own, the mother had no idea how to prepare her for menstruation. The student, who we'll call Cathy, had limited verbal ability, mild to moderate mental impairment, sensory sensitivities and many obsessive-compulsive rituals and routines.

Since Cathy already had some pubic hair, we knew that we had less than a year before the possible onset of her first period.The school nurse and I prepared a curriculum and a step-by-step plan based on her cognitive and physical capabilities, discussed our plan with the mother and asked her to keep an eye on her daughter's development while supporting our curriculum plan at home.

We introduced Cathy to the concept of menstruation with a story called Getting My Period. I also wrote an individualized story using her name and picture throughout, to be read and discussed at home with her mother. After that, we discussed the use of pads and actually practiced putting them in a pair of panties. This was a tabletop activity used with photo sequence cards to show the step-by-step process. Cathy practiced using the photo cards as a guideline.

We also introduced the concept of blood using a story called Blood Will Come, and even used red food coloring on sanitary pads to illustrate the menstrual blood. The food coloring on the pad looks remarkably like real menstrual blood, which was appropriate, because we wanted the "bloodied "pads to look as much like the real thing as possible. We then returned to practicing the sequence activity of putting in a clean, white pad, and carefully removing the dirty, red pad. We practiced folding and wrapping the dirty pad, throwing it into the appropriate trash receptacle, and finally, washing hands with soap and water. An activity booklet called I Wear Pads In My Panties helped to reinforce the pad sequence and was used as a demonstration of Cathy's comprehension of the concepts presented.

Our student was doing remarkably well with all the activities and concepts, but we knew it was time to practice actually wearing the pads in her underwear. We asked the mother to select a brand and type of pad, which would be best suited to her daughter. The mother had Cathy help her with this, bearing in mind that once a particular pad was selected they would need to stay with that brand and style indefinitely since Cathy had little tolerance for change. (People with autism become used to the feel, appearance and even brand name of a particular product and may have a very difficult time tolerating something different.)

Cathy was uncomfortable and reluctant at first to wear pads in her panties. But we started slowly, allowing her time to get used to the feel of the pads and the change in her bathroom routine. Eventually she was able to wear the pads all day for 5 days in a row. Even though she had not started her period yet, her mother would help her check the pads. ("No blood yet? That's okay, maybe blood will come tomorrow.")

We knew the day would come soon and occasionally asked the student if the blood came yet. We also knew that her mother was checking at home and would let us know when Cathy started her period. But we all missed her actual first day! Cathy began her period one weekend and told no one, not even her mother! She knew what she was supposed to do, began putting in the pads as she was taught and carefully managed her first day of her first period. When her mother discovered it the next day, she was astonished that her daughter had managed the situation totally on her own. We knew then that we had been successful because we had achieved acceptance of a new and unfamiliar routine.

Finally, I created a simple visual chart with pictures to help Cathy independently manage changing her pads in the school bathroom. The step-by- step directions and a pocket for holding her pad were discreetly contained in a folder, which she took with her to the bathroom. We had also instructed her to change her pads discreetly in the toilet stall with the door closed and not to tell others what she was doing. Once she knew exactly what to do, and no longer needed the folder, she began to carry a small cosmetic bag containing her pads to the bathroom. By the time she entered junior high, she carried a small, fashionable purse to the bathroom and changed her pads just like all the other girls at school.

We have since taught other girls about getting their periods and how to manage the monthly process themselves. These students, even those who are non-verbal and cognitively low but physically capable of managing the process, have learned to do so, discreetly and independently.

Not all girls, of course, are physically or cognitively capable of self-managing their monthly periods. But, I think it's important for instructors and parents to remember to teach as much as they can handle and empower them as much as possible. I have been repeatedly surprised at how well the students I've worked with have been able to meet and even surpass our expectations.

A mother whose daughter had severe disabilities, cognitive as well as physical, once asked me why or if she should even bother instructing her daughter when the girl wore a diaper and could never manage any part of this new process. I told her I believe we have an obligation to teach what we can and try to help them understand to the best of their ability. Even if we aren't sure how much of the curriculum a student can cognitively process, the goal is to facilitate as much independent functioning as they are capable of handling while also helping to reduce the fear and distress that often accompanies menstruation.

The goals and anticipated progression of skills for this unit:

- Student will understand the process of menstruation as a part of her own growth and development.

- Student will identify blood on a pad.

- Student will demonstrate the sequence of changing a pad with prompts.

- Student will tolerate wearing a sanitary pad.

- Student will recognize when blood comes and tell her parent.

- Student will change soiled sanitary napkin independently and dispose of them properly.

- Student will understand menstrual cramping and be able to tell a parent or teacher when cramps occur.

- Student will demonstrate discretion and modesty during her menstrual period.

The following activities and stories were created to help girls of varying cognitive and physical capabilities to understand menstruation and learn to self-manage the process of monthly periods efficiently, discreetly and independently, to the best of their ability.

The following story is a generic, introductory story about getting your period. It is often initially presented to a group of girls who are showing some signs of puberty but are approximately 1 to 2 years away from actually having a period. The menstruation unit typically builds, with more stories and activities added as students get older and closer to the onset of menstruation, and even after menstruation begins. I will often introduce this story to girls in the fourth grade.

↳ My body is changing. My body is growing bigger and taller. My breasts are growing bigger.

↳ Hair is growing on my privates and underarms. Soon I will have my period.

↳ When I have my period, blood will come from my privates, between my legs. This is okay.

↳ Blood will come from my privates for a few days and then it will stop.

↳ At first I might be scared and upset to see blood between my legs.

↳ But having a period is okay. I am not hurt when the blood comes from my privates.

↳

↳ All big girls, mommies and adult women have periods.

↳ A period usually happens every month. Blood will come out of my privates for five or six days, and then the blood will stop.

↳ A period is messy. Blood might get on my underwear and pants. Wearing pads in my panties will help.

↳ During my period, I will wear pads in my panties. Blood from my privates will go on the pads.

↳ When the pad becomes dirty with blood, I will take out the yucky, red pad in the bathroom and throw it away.

↳ I will put a clean, white pad in my panties. I will fold and wrap the old pad in toilet paper and throw it away.

↳ I always need to wash my hands after I change my pads. I will wash my hands after I throw away the yucky, red pad.

↳ I will change my pads in the bathroom with the door shut. I will change my pad when I use the toilet.

↳ My period will come every month. Mom will know when my period comes. Mom will help me know when I need to wear pads in my panties.

↳ Sometimes, I won't like my period. Sometimes, I will feel uncomfortable and sad when the blood comes.

↳ Sometimes, women are uncomfortable when they get their period. Mommy will help me when I am sad and uncomfortable with my period.

↳ I will feel better soon.

➥ I will be okay when I get my period.

➥ I am a big girl now. I will get my period like
　Mommy and other big girls.

➥ I will do a good job of wearing my pads. I will do
　a good job of changing my pads in the bathroom.

 **I will do a good job when I get my period and the blood comes.**

The Picture Communication Symbols copyright 1981-2002, Mayer-Johnson, Inc. Used with permission.

A fifth grade student learns about menstrual periods reading the story, Getting My Period with the author.

This story was written to explain in simple language what will happen during a period and why we need to wear pads. The story was originally made using some actual photos of panties, pads and "blood" for those students who may not understand abstract pictures. This is an example of how you can tailor a story to meet the specific needs of an individual. See figure.

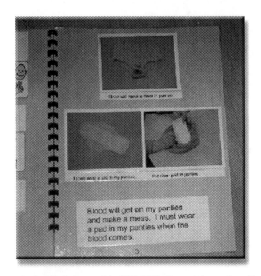

The Picture Communication Symbols copyright 1981-2002, Mayer-Johnson, Inc. Used with permission.

Some students need photo illustrations in order to understand the content of a story. This is an example of how you can use photos to accompany the story, Blood Will Come.

Blood Will Come

⇘ I am a big girl now. I will get my period every month and blood will come between my legs from my privates.

⇘ Blood will come every month. I don't like the blood, but I know it is okay when the blood comes.

⇘ Blood is supposed to come out between my legs when I have my period. The blood does not hurt me. I'm not sick. I'm fine.

⇘ The blood coming from my privates means I'm a big girl. I am becoming a woman, like my mommy.

⇘ The blood is called my period. The blood makes a mess. I need to wear pads in my panties when the blood comes.

⇘

🐦 I must wear pads when the blood comes. The blood will go on my pad, not on my panties.

🐦 Maybe the pads will feel strange and uncomfortable in my panties. Maybe I won't like the pads at first. But soon the pads will feel fine and I won't worry about them.

🐦 The pads will keep my panties clean when the blood comes. I must keep the pads in my panties when the blood comes.

🐦 The blood comes between my legs from my privates for about five days and then the blood will stop.

🐦 When the blood stops, I won't need to wear pads in my panties.

🐦 Soon the blood will come again. Then I will need to wear pads in my panties again.

🐦 I will be okay when I get my period and the blood comes.

I will do a good job of wearing pads in my panties when the blood comes.

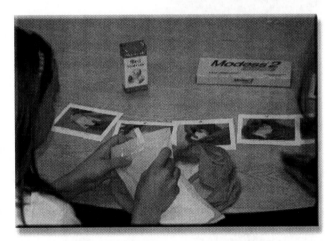

The following is a hands-on activity to help instill the concept of wearing and changing pads. This simple story has been created in a workbook form to allow students to read, write and color or as a reinforcement of the information learned.

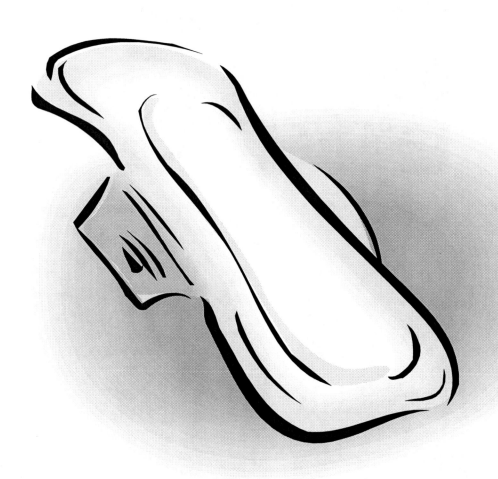

I Wear Pads in My Panties

1. Clean white pad
2. Pad goes in panties
3. Blood on pad
4. Yucky red pad comes out
5. Wrap pad. Don't touch blood
6. Throw pad away
7. Wash hands

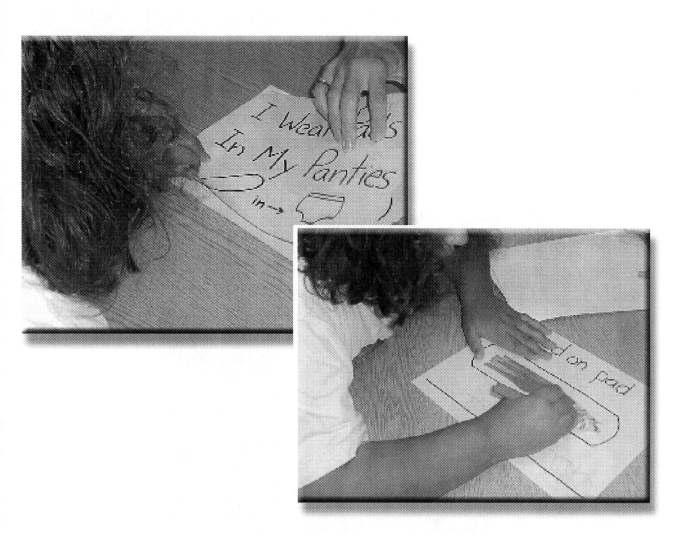

Because reading about sanitary pads and looking at pictures of sanitary pads is not the same as actually using them yourself, it is advisable for girls about to get their periods to learn how to physically handle the process of changing their pads. Initially, learning this process may require hand-over-hand assistance by an adult. Eventually, however, each girl needs to learn this process on her own, following the sequence independently.

We initially teach and practice the pad-changing sequence at a desk or table. We use a 12-photo set of sequence cards, real sanitary pads, a pair of underpants, toilet paper, red food coloring, a trash can, hand soap, and an available sink.

The student is instructed to put a clean, white pad into the pair of underpants and position the pad appropriately. An instructor applies red food coloring to the pad to simulate blood. (Note: It looks remarkably like actual blood as it appears on a sanitary pad.) We do this because if the students recognize what menstrual blood looks like on a pad, they will grow accustomed to it and less fearful when the process begins for real. The girl is then instructed to lift the soiled pad out of the panties, without touching the "blood," and then roll and wrap the pad in toilet paper. Finally she must throw the pad away and wash her hands with soap and water. Repeated practice may be necessary for mastery of the skill.

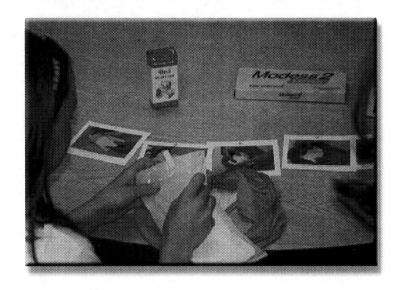

Changing Pads

12-step photo sequence cards:

1. Take sanitary pad out of package.

2. Pull off sticky strip.

3. Place clean pad into panties.

4. Press sticky side of pad to panties.

5. Fold wings around panties.

6. Blood goes on pad.

7. Take hold of the top end of the pad and pull up.

8. Carefully pull out pad from panties.
   Don't touch the blood!

9. Fold(or roll) the dirty pad.

10. Wrap the dirty pad with some toilet paper

11. Throw pad in trash can.

12. Wash hands with soap and water.

Once a student understands and accepts the process of wearing pads in her panties during her period, and has learned how to change her pads, she is now ready to learn how to follow the routine by herself in the bathroom. By creating a bathroom folder for each girl, a student can discreetly carry her pads to the bathroom. She will also have a step- by- step pictured guide to help her follow the procedure for changing her pads independently. As seen in the photo, a small envelope is laminated and velcroed inside the bathroom folder. The envelope contains the clean pad which the student will use. It's important to teach each student to be discreet and not open her folder until she is in the bathroom stall and ready to change her pad. It is highly recommended that the bathroom folder and the envelope for the pad be laminated for easy washing, since they will be used in a bathroom stall.

Once the student has mastered the step-by-step process on her own, and no longer needs the visual supports to help her change her pads independently, she can begin using a cosmetic bag or purse to carry her pad in when she goes to the bathroom to change. A small visual reminder card can be taken to the bathroom, if necessary, in her purse.

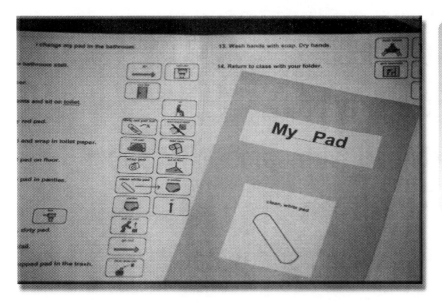

This sample bathroom folder was created using Boardmaker pictures (Mayer-Johnson Company, Inc.) which help to illustrate the step-by-step process.

Creating a Bathroom Folder

These are the suggested steps to have each student follow:

I take my folder with a pad to the bathroom when I have my period.

1. I go into the bathroom stall
2. I shut the door
3. I pull down my pants and sit on the toilet
4. I take out the dirty, red pad
5. I roll up the dirty pad and wrap it in toilet paper
6. I place the wrapped pad on the floor
7. I stick a clean, white pad on my panties
8. I pull up my panties and my pants
9. I flush the toilet
10. I pick up the wrapped, dirty pad
11. I leave the bathroom stall
12. I throw away the dirty, wrapped pad into the trash
13. I wash my hands with soap and water
14. I return to my class with my folder

I recommend that students develop their own personal stories about getting a period. Each girl's story will be specifically about her and can be sent home to be read and shared with her mother. It's important for mothers to have the opportunity to discuss the menstrual process with their daughters, and these personal stories invite parent participation while keeping the information consistent between home and school. In this way, teachers and parents work together to create and follow a plan designed for the individual child.

(Student's) Period

↳ (Student's name)'s body is changing. (Student) is growing bigger and taller. (Student's) breasts are growing bigger. (Student) is growing hair in her privates and her underarms. Soon (student) will get her period.

↳ When (student) has her period blood will come from her privates. This is okay. Blood will come from her privates for a few days and then it will stop.

↳ At first, I might be scared and upset when I see the blood. But having a period is okay. Blood is supposed to come from between my legs sometimes. I am not hurt when I have my period.

↳ All big girls, mommies and adult women have periods. My mommy gets a period too.

☞ A period comes every month. Blood will come out of my privates for five or six days, and then it will stop.

☞ A period is messy. Blood will get on my underwear and pants. I need to wear pads in my underpants so the blood won't get on my clothes.

☞ During my period, I will wear pads in my underpants. The blood will go onto the pads. The pads may feel funny in my underpants, but they will keep my panties clean.

☞ When the pads become yucky with blood, I will change them in the bathroom and put them in the trash. I will carefully remove my dirty pad and wrap it in toilet paper. Then, I will throw it away.

☞ I will put a clean, white pad in my underpants while I sit on the toilet. When I pull up my panties, my clean pad will stay in my underwear until I need to change it.

↳ I will change my pads in the bathroom with the door shut. I will change my pad when I use the toilet. I can do a good job of changing my pads.

↳ My period will come every month. Mom will know when my period comes and I will need to wear pads in my underpants.

↳ I might not like my period, but I will do a good job of changing my pads in the bathroom. I will do a good job when my period comes.

 I am a big girl now. I will get my period like Mom and other big girls. I will do a good job with my period!

As most women know, not all periods will be the same. Some periods will be light, and others will be heavy. There may be bloating, breast tenderness and irritability before or during our periods as well as menstrual cramps. The following story addresses the problem of menstrual cramps and can also serve as a format for explaining and helping students cope with other menstrual problems.

Sometimes I Have Cramps

↳ I'm a big girl now. I get my period like other big girls, women and my Mom.

↳ Sometimes, my periods feel okay. I feel a little uncomfortable, but my periods don't upset me.

↳ Sometimes, I may have cramps when I have my period. Cramps feel like pain down low in my tummy. Cramps are uncomfortable and can hurt.

↳ I don't like cramps. No one likes having cramps. Cramps make me feel bad and sad.

↳ I need to tell Mom and my teachers when I have cramps. Mom and my teachers will help me feel better.

➪ Mom might give me medicine to stop the cramps. Mom might do other things to help me when I have cramps.

➪ I will do a good job of telling Mom and my teachers when I have cramps. I will do a good job of taking care of my period.

Mom will help me when I have cramps. Soon, my cramps will go away and I will feel better.

Having a period is a private matter, and as such, we need to teach our students to keep this information private. This story helps girls understand that while it's okay to discuss wearing sanitary pads with a parent, guardian, or close personal friend, it's not appropriate to tell other students, staff members, strangers or even extended family.

My Period Is Private

↳ My period is a private matter.

↳ People don't need to know when I'm having my period.

↳ I don't tell people about my period and I don't tell people I'm wearing pads.

↳ It's okay to tell Mom and maybe an adult who helps me at school when I get my period.

↳ But I don't tell other adults, students or people I don't know about my period.

↳ It's usually not okay to talk about my period. My period is a private matter.

↳ Sometimes, a teacher or a girlfriend might ask me about my period. It's usually okay to talk to a teacher or a girlfriend about my period.

↪ Sometimes, a nurse will ask me about my period. It's okay to tell a nurse about my period.

↪ I don't tell boys about my period. Boys don't need to know about my period.

↪ If I need help with my period or I am worried about my period, I will tell Mom or a teacher.

My period is a private matter. I don't tell students or most people about my period.

TOUCHING AND PERSONAL SAFETY

Understanding and demonstrating appropriate touching is the first step toward promoting personal safety

Teaching About Touching and Personal Safety

Personal safety is a real concern for many parents and teachers of children with special needs, including autism. Although it is not known exactly how many people with disabilities are molested and sexually or physically abused, it is agreed by most that the percentages are high. It has been estimated that 80 percent of girls with disabilities and 30 to 50 percent of disabled boys are sexually abused by the time they reach the age of 18(Harvard Education Letter, April, 1999). These are shocking statistics, yet some sources believe the actual numbers in both cases to be even higher. And during the lifetime of a person with disabilities, the likelihood of abuse may rise further.

Although we would never intentionally put our students or children in a potentially dangerous situation, abuse of any kind can occur anywhere. It's not realistic or possible to protect our students or children 24 hours a day. But, parents and teachers have found that the best way to protect children from the danger of abuse is to educate them and teach them about what they should do. This is especially true, albeit a more challenging task, for students with disabilities.

The information presented in this unit should be learned as a life long skill and as such, revisited and reviewed regularly. Some of the skills may, in fact, be life-saving with regards to personal safety. Since it is often very difficult for our students and children to communicate when something wrong or hurtful has occurred, parents and teachers need to be alert to any changes on the part of a child which may indicate abuse, and make every effort to help them communicate any such events to us.

Personal safety issues go hand in hand with learning about modesty, independence and dealing with sexual situations. The following stories and activities cover the topics of touching, talking about sex or sex related topics, strangers, molestation and abuse. Much of this information has been the driving force behind the development of this curriculum because, ultimately, we want our students and children to be safe.

The goals and anticipated progression of skills for this unit:

- The student will be able to identify the "private areas".

- The student will identify appropriate and inappropriate places to touch another person.

- The student will identify appropriate and inappropriate places to be touched.

- The student will demonstrate the appropriate response of "no touching" or "stop touching" when touched inappropriately.

- The student will demonstrate how to tell a trusted adult if touched inappropriately by another person.

- The student will understand the word "stranger" and differentiate between familiar people and strangers.

- The student will demonstrate how to tell a trusted adult if a stranger talks to him, tries to take him away or gives him something.

- The student will demonstrate understanding of personal topics, which he/she can not talk about with others.

This is a vitally important story because it explains the concept of personal safety in simple language that students with a wide range of disabilities can understand. Some of the information is presented as an absolute. I don't typically use the words always and never in my stories, but this type of story is an exception. Since it is difficult for so many autistic students to 'read' people and understand the intentions of others, I have found it is easier to give them very specific rules regarding their safety.

Sometimes People Touch You

▷ Sometimes, people will touch you.

▷ If people touch you on the arm, shoulder, hand or back, it is usually okay.

▷ If people touch you and it is not okay, you need to say, "No, don't touch me."

▷ It is <u>not</u> okay for people to touch your private areas. My swimsuit or my underwear covers my private areas.

▷ It is not okay for people to touch my private areas even when I'm wearing my clothes.

▷ Sometimes, a doctor, a nurse or my mom may need to touch my private areas. That's usually okay.

↳ But other people should <u>not</u> touch my private areas.

↳ If someone touches my private areas I need to tell them, "No, touching!" I need to tell a teacher and my parents when someone touches my private areas.

↳ It is <u>never</u> okay for a student, friend or adult to touch my private areas.

↳ Kissing is also touching. It is okay for my family to kiss me.

↳ It is <u>not</u> okay for students, friends or other adults to kiss me. If someone kisses me, I need to say, "No, don't kiss me."

↳ I need to tell my teacher and Mom or Dad if someone won't stop kissing me.

↳ It is <u>never</u> okay for people to touch my private areas. I will say, "No, don't touch me."

I will do a good job of telling a teacher and my parents when someone touches my private areas.

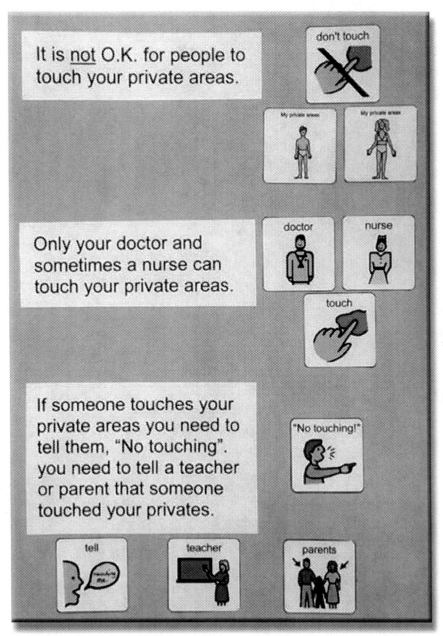

It is <u>not</u> O.K. for people to touch your private areas.

Only your doctor and sometimes a nurse can touch your private areas.

If someone touches your private areas you need to tell them, "No touching". you need to tell a teacher or parent that someone touched your privates.

The Picture Communication Symbols copyright 1981-2002, Mayer-Johnson, Inc. Used with permission.

Besides teaching students the rules regarding their own personal safety, we need to explain that these rules apply to everyone. This story explains that no one's personal safety should be violated and everyone should follow the same rules.

Touching Others

↳ Sometimes, it's okay to touch people.

↳ Sometimes, it's not okay to touch people.

↳ It is okay to touch friends on the arm, on the back, or on the shoulder.

↳ It is usually okay to shake hands with people.

↳ It is usually okay to hug family members.

↳ Sometimes, it's okay to hug teachers and friends.

↳ But sometimes, people don't want a hug. If you aren't sure, you need to ask someone for a hug.

↳ If someone doesn't want a hug and says, "No," I won't give a hug.

↳

↳ It is <u>not</u> okay to hug strangers or most adults. It is <u>not</u> okay to ask strangers or most adults for a hug.

↳ Sometimes, people will tell you not to touch them. It's important to remember, don't touch if someone says, "No touching."

↳ The areas on our bodies covered by a swim suit or underwear are private areas. We <u>never</u> touch someone's private areas!

↳ It is wrong to touch a person's private areas. People may be angry and upset if someone touches their private areas. It is <u>never</u> okay to touch people's private areas!

↳ Kissing is touching. It is okay to kiss Mom or Dad and other family members.

↳ It is <u>not</u> okay to kiss friends, students, or other adults.

 People may get mad and upset if you kiss them. It is wrong to kiss people at school. It is wrong to kiss people when they say, "No kiss."

I will do a good job of touching people the right way. I will remember to only touch people on the arm, hand, back or shoulder.

If someone says, "No touching," I will remember not to touch them.

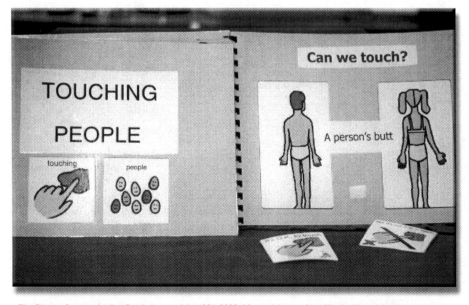

The Picture Communication Symbols copyright 1981-2002, Mayer-Johnson, Inc. Used with permission.

Can We Touch? Activity Booklet

The following activity is designed as an evaluation or reinforcement of learned skills. Students using this activity booklet must determine whether or not it is okay to touch someone. Each question is presented individually and students respond either verbally or non-verbally with a picture response if touching is allowed. I often use velcroed picture responses which can be placed appropriately on the pages.

I wanted to present touching rules to live by. There will always be exceptions to these rules, but since your students may not understand the exceptions, it is better to present this information as an absolute. For example, it may be acceptable on occasion to touch someone's head or leg, but it is typically inappropriate to do so, therefore, I teach that it's not okay to touch those areas.

These are rules that students need to learn and demonstrate an understanding of. It may be necessary to practice the activity repeatedly before mastery is achieved.

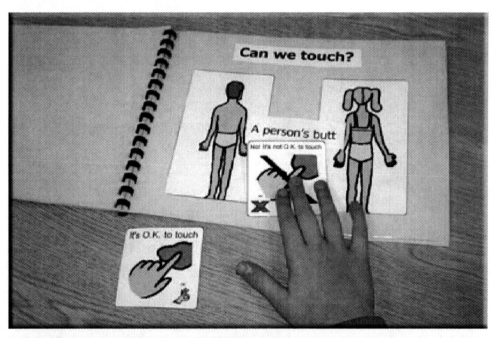

The Picture Communication Symbols copyright 1981-2002, Mayer-Johnson, Inc. Used with permission.

The velcroed responses for this story are "It's usually okay to touch," or "No! Don't touch!" Keeping the information and responses simple increases student comprehension and encourages appropriate responses.

Can We Touch?

1. An arm?

Yes, It's usually okay to touch

2. A person's head or face?

No! It's usually not okay

3. A hand?

Yes, It's usually okay to touch

4. A back?

Yes, It's usually okay to touch

5. Private areas on boys?

No! It's not okay to touch!

6. Private areas on girls?

No! It's not okay to touch!

7. A person's butt?

No! It's not okay to touch!

8. A shoulder?

Yes, It's usually okay to touch

9. A person's legs and feet?

No! It's usually not okay

Where Can People Touch Me?
Activities to demonstrate student comprehension

It's not enough to explain to our students where it is and isn't okay for people to touch. Students also need to demonstrate their understanding of this concept. The following activities facilitate this. Either abstract pictures or actual digital pictures of individual students may be used.

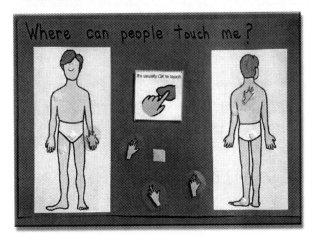 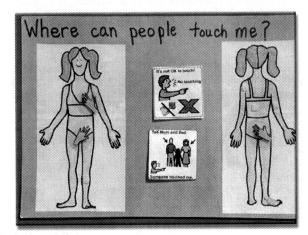

The Picture Communication Symbols copyright 1981-2002, Mayer-Johnson, Inc. Used with permission.

In the examples, an abstract picture of a gender-specific student in underwear is shown. The figures are laminated, as are the small hand cutouts. Velcro is attached to each hand. Several small pieces of Velcro are attached to the body pictures as possible areas to place the hands. During separate trials, instruct students to use the hands to indicate where it is okay for people to touch. And where it is not okay for people to touch. After each trial, students may choose among three non-verbal responses: "It's usually okay to touch," or "No, It's not okay to touch," and "Tell Mom and Dad someone touched me." The last two non-verbal responses should be used together.

If students have a hard time understanding that the abstract pictures are supposed to represent them, it may be necessary to take an actual picture of them (fully clothed) to use in this exercise. It is also important to note that students need be taught the inappropriateness of touch whether they are clothed or not. In other words, it is not okay to be touched in private areas fully clothed, in underwear or naked. Abstract pictures of students in underwear help students identify private areas, and therefore make appropriate choices during the instruction trials. Actual photos of students, fully clothed, help them connect the concept of touching to themselves.

In all activities, communication boards or voice output devices may be necessary. The pictured responses used may be changed to meet the language comprehension and communication needs of individual students. However, the language and pictures used should remain consistent for individual students otherwise there may be confusion and difficulty understanding the task or information.

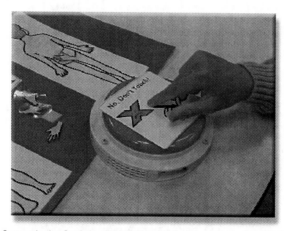

The Picture Communication Symbols copyright 1981-2002, Mayer-Johnson, Inc. Used with permission.

My Touching Rules

A personal story for individual students to use at home

⇘ Sometimes, it is okay to touch others. I can touch people on the arm, back, shoulder or hands.

⇘ People can touch me on my hands, my shoulder, my arms and my back.

⇘ Sometimes, it's <u>not</u> okay to touch others. I don't touch people on their underwear, private areas or the bottom.

⇘ People can't touch me on my underwear, my private areas or bottom.

⇘ If someone touches me in a private place, I need to say, "No" or "Stop it," and I will tell Mom and Dad.

⇘ It is wrong to touch people on their privates. I will <u>never</u> touch people's privates.

 My privates belong to me. Only I can look at and touch my privates. I will do a good job of touching people the right way. I will gently touch people on their arms, shoulders, backs and hands.

I will <u>not</u> let people touch my private areas. I will say, "No" and tell Mom and Dad. I will do a good job of following my touching rules.

Picture It computer program copyright 1994-2002, Slater Software, Inc. Used with permission.

It can be difficult for students with autism and other developmental delays to understand what's appropriate to talk about. Subjects such as sex and private matters, are generally taboo to discuss in mixed company and most typically developing children tend to intuit what they can and cannot talk by checking the reactions of others when they're uncertain about a topic. Since our students often have difficulties reading the reactions of others, they find it harder to gauge if what they say is appropriate or not. As such, I find it is best to teach them to simply avoid discussing sex and private matters in public.

Talking About Sex and Private Areas

↳ Sometimes, we think about sex and private areas. It's okay to think about private areas, but it's <u>not</u> okay to talk about private areas.

↳ I could get into trouble if I talked about my private areas. My family, friends, students, teachers, and other adults would be upset if I talked to them about private areas.

↳ I can't talk about my private areas or anyone else's private areas.

↳ I can't talk about private areas at school, at home, outside, on a bus, in a car, in a store or anywhere.

↳ Private areas are personal. We should not talk about our private areas or anyone else's private areas.

✎ Sometimes, I may need to talk to a doctor, a nurse, or my mom about my private areas because they want to know important information, and they want me to be safe and healthy.

✎ If I have pain or blood in my private areas, I would tell my teacher, the nurse, my mom and sometimes a doctor. It's important to tell someone when I have pain in my privates.

✎ But, my private areas are my business. I don't discuss my private areas with other people. I only talk to a trusted adult when it's important and if I have pain or blood in my private areas.

✎ Other people's private areas are their business. I will <u>never</u> talk about other people's private areas.

✎ If someone wants me to talk about private areas, I will ignore them, walk away or say, "No".

↳ If someone keeps talking to me about private areas or sex, I will tell a teacher and my parents.

↳ It's okay to think about private areas and sex, but it's not okay to talk about private areas.

 I will do a good job and <u>not</u> talk about private areas to friends, students, and other adults.

Teaching the concept of stranger danger is always a tricky one for our students. Many students with autism don't differentiate between people they know and can trust and those they don't know and shouldn't trust. I find it best to keep the rules simple, consistent, and easy to understand without worrying about the explanations.

I Don't Know Strangers

↳ Strangers are people I don't know.

↳ I might see many strangers. Sometimes Mom or Dad will talk to a stranger. Sometimes a stranger will smile at me and I can smile back.

↳ But I don't know strangers, so I won't talk to a stranger or go to a stranger. Strangers are people I don't know.

↳ It is usually not okay to talk to strangers. Sometimes I can talk to a stranger if I'm with Mom and Dad and they think it's okay.

↳ It is <u>never</u> okay to be alone with a stranger or go anywhere with a stranger.

↳ A stranger may act nice and pretend to know me, but sometimes, a stranger might try to hurt me.

↳

- I don't know if a stranger is a good person or a bad person. I know that I must <u>not</u> go anywhere with a stranger.

- If a stranger tries to talk to me and wants me to go with him or her, I will say, "No!" and run to my parents. I will always tell Mom and Dad when a stranger talks to me.

- Strangers can be dangerous!

- I will <u>never</u> go in a stranger's car unless Mom and Dad say it's okay.

- I will <u>never</u> take food, toys or anything from a stranger.

 **I will always tell Mom and Dad and my teachers when a stranger talks to me or touches me.**

Physical abuse can be one of many concerns regarding students with special needs. Just as many typically developing students might not report physical abuse, it is just as likely or more often the case that special needs students won't either. In some situations, they can't. We need to explain to our students that physical abuse is a bad and dangerous situation and that they need to immediately report any incident to at least three people (ex: mom, dad and a teacher). We also need to provide them with the necessary communication supplements to tell us. Here is a story that addresses this difficult topic.

It's <u>Not</u> Okay to Hurt Me

🖐 Sometimes when people touch me, it hurts. If someone bumps, hits or grabs me, it might hurt. It's <u>not</u> okay to hurt me.

🖐 People might not mean to hurt me. Sometimes, it's an accident and they will say, "Sorry."

🖐 Sometimes, people might hurt me because they're angry and upset. It's okay to be upset but it's <u>not</u> okay to hurt me.

🖐 When someone hits, pinches, bites me or pulls my hair, that is <u>not</u> okay. That hurts me and hurting is bad.

🖐 I need to tell my teachers and my mom and dad if someone hurts me. Any time someone hurts me, I need to tell adults who can help me.

➯ If someone tries to hurt me, I need to say, "Stop that!" or "Don't hurt me." It is <u>not</u> okay to hurt me.

➯ If someone hurts me, I need to tell an adult and show them where I got hurt. Sometimes, I might get a bruise or a bump where someone hurts me. I will show an adult the bump or bruise.

➯ Sometimes, someone who hurts me may say, "Don't tell." I know I must tell my teacher and my Mom and Dad.

➯ I must always tell an adult and Mom and Dad when someone hurts me. I won't wait. I will tell right away when someone hurts me.

 It is <u>not</u> okay to hurt me. Hurting is bad. I will remember to <u>always</u> tell an adult I know, and Mom and Dad, if someone hurts me.

Creating Question-Answer Personal Safety Cards

The following question-answer cards can be made to use in group discussions or one-on-one with a student. I typically put the question on one side and the answer(s) on the other. I recommend creating these cards with visual supports, such as Boardmaker Picture Communication Symbols.

Personal Safety Question-Answer Cards:

1. Where can I touch people?

Answer: It's usually okay to touch on the hand, on the back, on the shoulder, and on the arm.

2. Where can people touch me?

Answer: It's usually okay to touch me on my hand, on my shoulder, on my back and on my arm.

3. Where do I never touch people?

Answer: I never touch people in their private areas.

4. Where should people never touch me?

Answer: People should never touch my private areas even when I have clothes on.

5. What should I do if someone touches my private areas?

Answer: I need to tell them "No!" and "Stop!" I need to tell Mom, Dad and a teacher that someone touched my private area.

6. What should I do if someone hurts me or tries to hurt me?

Answer: I need to tell Mom, Dad and a trusted adult right away, and show them where I was hurt.

7. Who can I kiss?

Answer: It is okay to kiss my parents, my grandparents, my brothers or sisters and other family members on the face. It's not okay for me to kiss students, friends, or any other adults.

8. Is it okay for people to kiss me?

Answer: It's okay for my parents, and other family members to kiss me on my face. It's not okay for any students, friends or other adults to kiss me.

9. Is it okay for a stranger to talk to me?

Answer: It's okay only if Mom, Dad or a trusted adult is with me and they think it's okay.

10. Is it okay to go someplace with a stranger?

Answer: It's only okay to go someplace with a stranger if Mom or Dad are with me. I never go anywhere with a stranger by myself. I never go anywhere with a stranger without Mom or Dad.

My Sentences About Touching Worksheet

The following activity is a fill-in-the blank worksheet for students to do at home or at school to reinforce the rules of touching. This activity allows students to demonstrate comprehension of the information taught. Students can either write in the correct responses or choose the appropriate picture response and glue them into the spaces provided. Visual supports are recommended for this activity.

My Sentences About Touching

1. It's okay for people to touch...

      my_____ and my _____.

2. It's not okay for people to touch my...

      _____.

3. If someone touches any of my private areas, I need to say...

      _____.

4. My private areas are those places on my body which are usually covered by my...

      _____.

5. If someone touches any of my private areas, I need to tell...

      _____.

6. My private areas belong to...

      _____.

MASTURBATION

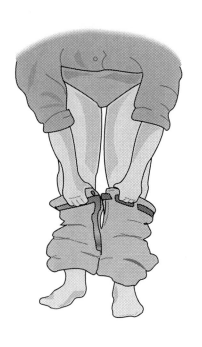

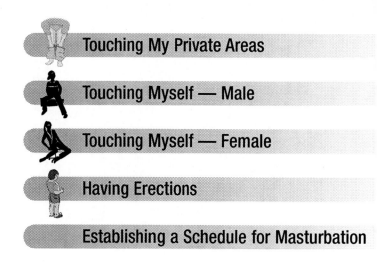

Touching My Private Areas

Touching Myself — Male

Touching Myself — Female

Having Erections

Establishing a Schedule for Masturbation

Dealing with masturbation in a calm and accepting manner promotes appropriate social behavior. Coordinating a plan at home for acceptable masturbation prevents socially unacceptable behavior.

Addressing Masturbation

Masturbation is a private, sexual behavior that most parents never even talk about with their children. For children and adults with special needs, it's often considered a problem behavior, and most people are shocked and upset when they see others masturbating, and their reactions towards students with special needs are no exception.

With all the social and moral taboos regarding masturbation, many people don't realize it is a natural behavior. In fact, it's not uncommon for young children and even infants to masturbate. When children discover the pleasurable sensations it can produce, they will continue to engage in it, often without any thought as to its appropriateness. Eventually, most children correctly label masturbation as a private matter and learn not to discuss it or do it in public.

But students with special needs, particularly those with autism or mental impairments, are not as likely to be embarrassed by masturbation or to understand the social and moral taboos attached to it. Sometimes, negative attention merely exacerbates a situation, and a student will continue the inappropriate behavior. Other times, adults mistakenly believe that masturbation is a behavior a child will soon tire of and stop on his or her own. This is seldom the case, however, and if a student is masturbating even occasionally in public, whether he's unaware of the reactions of others or doing so despite the negative attention of others, responsible teachers and parents must immediately address the behavior.

To do so, it is important to have an appropriate attitude about masturbation and to approach the subject with maturity and calm understanding. Rather than simply telling children to stop the behavior, teachers and parents should discuss why it is inappropriate to do so in public and tell them where and when it is okay to engage in the private activity.

Several years ago, I had a student with autism who masturbated frequently. He was a seventh grade boy who was entering puberty. His parents, distressed by the behavior, had forbidden any masturbation at home, and his teacher, appropriately, did not allow him to masturbate in the classroom. Unfortunately, as pubescent boys often do, he continued the pleasurable activity, only he did it in the most inappropriate places: the school bathroom, the playground, the school bus, the locker room, the school hallway and even at the end of the driveway in front of his house. Not only had his masturbation behavior become problematic, it threatened to lead to more serious situations involving his personal safety.

In a discussion with the boy's parents, it was decided that he should be allowed to masturbate at home in the privacy of his bedroom or bathroom. His parents and teachers explained that he could only do it in his bedroom or bathroom with the door closed and that he shouldn't discuss his masturbation with anyone. From then on, the student masturbated only at home, according to his own schedule, and no one was obviously aware of it.

This story illustrates the importance of taking an informative approach rather than a punitive one, and simply teaching the rules and boundaries that apply when students engage in this behavior.

Also, although it is essential to teach students the appropriate times and places to masturbate, teachers may not want to introduce this curriculum to students who are not actively exhibiting the behavior. In other words, we don't want to teach our students to masturbate.

The goals and anticipated progression of skills for this unit:

- Student will understand that masturbation is a very private behavior.

- Student will identify appropriate places and circumstances for masturbation.

- Student will understand the consequences for touching self or masturbating in public.

- Student will recognize non-verbal cues to stop masturbating or touching self inappropriately.

- Student will understand about erections and ejaculations and learn to manage his behavior privately and appropriately.

It's not uncommon for young, pre-pubescent students to masturbate. They may not be especially aware of their genitals or realize that their behavior is inappropriate. They may be masturbating because it calms them down or simply feels good. Regardless of the reasons, if it becomes problematic, it should be addressed. The following is a generic story about masturbating for either gender. It can be used with young or older students.

Touching My Private Areas

↳ It is okay to touch, rub, or scratch most areas on your body while others are looking.

↳ I can scratch my head, rub my arm, touch my legs or feet while others are watching.

↳ It is not okay to touch, scratch, or rub my private areas when students, parents, children or other adults can see me.

↳ My private areas are the places on my body which are usually covered by my underwear.

↳ When people are watching, it is <u>not</u> okay to touch and rub my penis, my bottom or between my legs, even when I have clothes on.

↳ When people are watching, it is <u>not</u> okay to touch my breasts, my bottom or between my legs, even when I have clothes on.

↳ People will be upset and offended if they see me rub my private areas. I may be embarrassed if they see me rub my private areas. It is not okay to touch private areas when people are watching.

↳ If I need to touch my private areas I will make sure I'm alone in a room with the door shut.

↳ It is okay to fold my hands on my lap, fold my arms, or place my hands at my side. It is not okay to put my hands between my legs when people are watching.

 I will remember <u>not</u> to touch my private areas when people are watching.

Even though this curriculum does not address sex and intercourse, masturbation is discussed because it is typically the first sex act a child will experience and continue. In the case of pubescent boys, erections and ejaculations are a natural part of their sexual development. It becomes essential that young men with special needs understand and learn to manage their personal sexual activities. The following story should be used one-on-one with a pubescent boy who is masturbating on a regular basis.

Touching Myself

A story about male masturbation

🔖 It is okay for you to touch your own body.

🔖 It is okay to touch your own hands, legs, arms, head, face, back and feet when people are watching.

🔖 It is <u>not</u> okay to touch your private areas when people are watching.

🔖 Your private areas are your bottom, your penis and your testicles.

🔖 It is okay to touch your private areas when you are alone in your bedroom or in your bathroom with the door shut.

🔖 No one should see you touching your private areas.

🔖 Only you can touch your private areas. Sometimes, it will feel good to touch yourself.

⤷ Teenage boys and adult men sometimes rub their penises. This is okay. But you must be alone when you touch your penis.

⤷ It is <u>not</u> okay to touch and rub your penis when other people are watching.

⤷ It is only okay to touch and rub your penis when you are alone in your bedroom or bathroom with the door shut.

⤷ Sometimes when you rub your penis, it gets bigger. Sometimes, something called semen will come out of your penis. This is called an ejaculation. This is okay.

⤷ Rubbing and touching your penis is a private matter. You should not talk to people about it. You do not need to tell your parents or anyone.

⤷ If your penis hurts or if blood comes from your penis, then you need to tell a parent and a doctor.

⤷ But, your penis, testicles and bottom are your private areas. Remember, your private areas belong to you. Only you can touch and look at your private areas.

We may not typically think of girls when we discuss masturbation, but, in fact, girls are as likely to masturbate as boys. The following story should be used one-on-one with a female student who is masturbating on a regular basis.

Touching Myself

A story about female masturbation

⇘ It is okay for you to touch your own body.

⇘ It is okay to touch your own hands, arms, head face and feet when people are watching.

⇘ It is <u>not</u> okay to touch your private areas when people are watching.

⇘ My private areas are my breasts, bottom and vagina. My private areas are places on my body which are covered by my underwear as well as other clothing.

⇘ It is okay for me to touch my private areas only when I am alone and people are not watching.

⇘ I can touch my private areas when I am alone in my bedroom or bathroom with the door shut.

⇘

↳ No one should see me touch my private areas.

↳ Only I may touch my private areas.

↳ Sometimes, it will feel good to touch myself. Girls and women sometimes touch their own private areas. This is okay.

↳ It is not okay to touch and rub my private areas when other people are watching.

↳ It is only okay to touch and rub my private areas when I am alone in my bedroom or bathroom with the door shut.

↳ Touching or rubbing my breasts or between my legs is a private matter. I don't talk to people about it. I don't tell Mom or Dad or anyone.

↳ If my breasts or vagina hurt or if it hurts to pee, I will tell Mom or my doctor.

➦ My breasts, vagina and bottom are my private areas. People must not see me touch my private areas.

 I will remember that my private areas belong to me. I am the only one who may touch and look at my private areas.

At some point young men begin to have erections. This is not necessarily something they can control. They may experience nighttime ejaculations or "wet dreams," and it may be confusing or frightening for them. The following story can help young men understand about erections and learn to manage them privately and appropriately.

Having Erections

↳ Sometimes, I have erections.

↳ All grown men and big boys have erections, and I get erections too.

↳ When I have an erection, my penis grows big and points forward.

↳ It's okay to have erections when I'm alone in my bedroom or bathroom.

↳ It's not okay to have erections when other people are near me.

↳ If I get an erection at school, I can go to a bathroom and wait until my erection goes down.

↳ I don't want people to see my erection or see me touch my penis.

☞ I don't tell people when I'm having an erection. An erection is a private matter. I don't talk about erections.

☞ It's okay to touch and rub my penis when I'm alone in my bedroom or bathroom with the door shut.

☞ Sometimes, I may want to touch and rub my penis when I have an erection. That's okay, but I must be alone in my bedroom or bathroom with the door shut.

☞ Sometimes when I have an erection, my penis may have an ejaculation. Then, semen will come out of my penis. This is okay.

☞ But, having an ejaculation can be messy. I will need to clean up the messy ejaculation. I can wipe my penis with toilet paper or wash myself in my bathroom.

↪ Sometimes, I may have an ejaculation in bed when I'm sleeping. I can ask my mom to wash my messy sheets if I have an ejaculation at night.

I am a big boy and sometimes my penis has erections and ejaculations. I will do a good job of keeping my erections and ejaculations private.

As surprising and awkward as this may seem to teachers and parents, young adolescent males typically need a regular outlet for their physical needs to avoid embarrassing and sometimes painful erections. Typically developing males learn that erections become a part of their lives and they may feel the need to relieve their physical needs in private with masturbation.

One mother of a teenage boy with autism found that establishing a schedule and routine for her son's masturbation kept his behavior discreet and manageable. Having a schedule appealed to this young man because he lived by and insisted on routines. The schedule helped to control his urges, since his masturbating had already become problematic, and it ultimately maintained his privacy. According to his schedule, this young man would typically masturbate in his bedroom twice a week before school. As part of his routine he would always close his bedroom door. He had a special lotion and pillow he used which were always kept in his room in a special place. He would sometimes look at a woman's fashion magazine, which he also had in his room. These objects were always kept in his room. His private routine prevented him from masturbating anywhere else, and although his parents were aware of the routine, it was never discussed because he had learned to be private about his masturbation. This method worked well for this young man, but this may not be the case for all young men with autism. Each person's needs are unique and teachers and parents need to work together to develop the best management plan for each individual.

The following story and schedule is an example that may help young men learn to control their sexual urges and establish an appropriate routine for managing masturbation. It should only be used with young men who need to establish a schedule or routine for existing masturbation behavior. I use the term "masturbate" in this story, but if a student is unfamiliar with a word, simpler language may be substituted.

My Private Routine

Establishing a Schedule for Masturbation

↳ Sometimes, I need to masturbate.

↳ Masturbating is okay, but I need to be alone in my bedroom or my bathroom with the door shut when I masturbate.

↳ Masturbating is a private matter. No one needs to know if I masturbate. No one should see me masturbate.

↳ I can decide what days and times I will masturbate. I need to be sure that I am alone when I masturbate. I will pick a time when I can be alone in my bedroom or bathroom at home.

1. I need to be alone in my bedroom or bathroom.

2. I need to close the door to the room so no one will see me.

237

3. I will get the things I use when I masturbate.

4. If anyone knocks on my door, I will tell them I'm busy. I won't open the door.

5. When I'm finished masturbating, I will clean my penis with a towel. I will put the towel in the laundry hamper.

6. I might wash my penis with water if it feels sticky.

7. I will put all my clothes back on before I open the door and leave the room.

8. I won't tell anyone about my masturbating. Only I need to know about my masturbating. Masturbating is my private routine.

Summary

I hope that this curriculum will serve as an example of how to create, supplement and modify instruction for teaching the necessary information in this book. Since the circumstances and needs for each individual student will vary, I hope some of these activities will give you the necessary ideas for creating the best curriculum for your students. Remember to use visual supports whenever possible when teaching this curriculum. Visual supports, as well as other communication aids, will help students comprehend and express information. Repeated presentation of this instruction and much practice will allow students to learn how to successfully take care of themselves.

References and Resources

Enkoji, M.S., *System often overlooks sex assaults on disabled*, The Sacramento Bee, January 11, 1998.

Giangreco, M., et al, (1993) *Choosing Options and Accommodations for Children(COACH) A Guide to Planning Inclusive Education,* Paul H. Brookes Publishing Co, Baltimore, MD.

Grandin, T., (1993) *Thinking In Pictures*, Vintage Books, division of Random House, Inc., New York.

Gray, C., (1994/2000) *The New Social Stories Book, Illustrated Edition*, Future Horizons, Inc. Arlington, Texas.

Kelly, K., "Developmentally Disabled Students Need Sex Ed, Too" Harvard Education Letter, March/April 1999, vol. 15, #2, Harvard Graduate School of Education, www.edletter.org.

As I stated throughout this book, it is important to use visual supports with the materials in this curriculum. Many of the materials used to create this curriculum, which are illustrated throughout this booklet, were made using pictures from the Mayer-Johnson Boardmaker Picture Communication Symbols. I highly recommend this program for a number of reasons. The Boardmaker computer program has 6,000 possible pictures, including addendum pictures, in its current library. Many of the pictures needed to cover the sensitive topics in this curriculum can be found in the Boardmaker library. The Boardmaker program is easy to use and the pictures can be formatted in a variety of ways to suit many communication needs.

Mayer-Johnson, Inc.
P.O. Box 1579
Solana Beach, CA 92075-7579
U.S.A.
Phone: 800-588-4548 or 858-550-0084
FAX: 858-550-0449
Email: mayerj@mayer-johnson. com
Website: www.mayer-johnson. com

The Don Johnston Company produces the Write Outloud computer software as well as other excellent products for assistive technology.

Don Johnston, Inc.
26799 W. Commerce Drive
Volo, IL 60073
Phone: 800-999-4660 or 847-740-0749
Fax: 847-740-7326
www.donjohnston.com

The Slater Software Company produces the Picture It and Pix Writer programs. Picture It is a picture supported computer literacy program and Pix Writer is a talking word-processing program which allows students to easily read and write with picture supports.

Slater Software, Inc.
351 Badger Lane
Guffey, CO 80820
Phone: 877-306- 6968 or 719-479-2255
Fax: 719-479-2254
Email: info@slatersoftware.com
www.slatersoftware.com

The Attainment Company produces several instructor guides for teaching sexuality and hygiene skills to students with disabilities. Much of their sex education curriculum is written for teenage through adult-age students. Many of the pictures they use in their products are realistic line drawings, which may be more suitable for students who can't understand abstract pictures.

Attainment Company, Inc.
P.O. Box 930160
Verona, Wisconsin 53593-0160
Phone: 800-327-4269
Fax: 800-942-3865
www.AttainmentCompany.com

The Ablenet Company produces many switches, such as the Big Mack, and other assistive technology equipment for students with physical and communicative challenges. The Big Mack switch is a single message(up to 20 seconds) voice output device. It is easy to program and use.

Ablenet, Inc.
1081 Tenth Avenue S.E.,
Minneapolis, MN 55414-1312
Phone: 800-322-0956
Fax: 612-379-9143
www.ablenetinc.com

The Cheap Talk 8 is an inexpensive, easy to program and use voice output device marketed by the Enabling Devices-Toys for Special Children, Inc. Company.

Enabling Devices- Toys for Special Children, Inc.
385 Warburton Avenue
Hastings-on-Hudson, NY 10706
Phone: 914-478-0960
Fax: 914-478-7030

The Superhawk voice output device is marketed by Adamlab-MB Products. The Superhawk is relatively easy to program. It contains 72 levels and up to 13 different overlay dimensions. It is an excellent device for using with several different students or groups of students. It can accommodate a variety of needs and topics.

Adamlab- MB Products
555 E. Long Lake Road
Mailstop PMB-337
Troy, Michigan 48098
Phone: 248-362-9603
Fax: 248-362-9606
www.adamlab.com

Dynavox Systems, Inc. produces the DigiVox2 voice output device. DigiVox 2 is a device which is versatile and easy to use. It has up to 18 minutes of recording capacity with several levels and dimensions to choose from.

Dynavox Systems, Inc.
2100 Wharton Street
Pittsburg, PA 15203
Phone: 888-697-7332
www.dynavoxsys.com

Using A Urinal

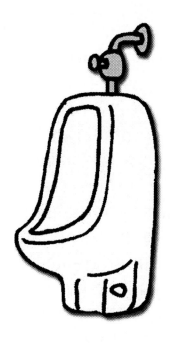

An additional story for young men on the proper use of urinals.

Using a urinal is not a difficult task, if a student knows how to urinate appropriately in a toilet. The difficulty in using a urinal has to do primarily with modesty. It is difficult to be private when using a urinal and there is a specific etiquette to using a urinal properly. Because urinals are open and typically exposed to whoever enters the bathroom, it becomes necessary to demonstrate as much privacy as possible despite being in a less than private environment. When we first teach boys how to use a toilet and urinate, we often teach them to drop pants and underwear to the floor. This is okay in a closed stall, but totally inappropriate when using a urinal. It is not only embarrassing and socially inappropriate, but it may compromise a person's personal safety. This modesty and discretion must also be demonstrated when urinating next to someone else. It is very inappropriate to watch someone urinating. We need to remind our students that it is not okay to look at someone's privates-his genitals-even when he is urinating next to us. Our young men and boys need to demonstrate as much discretion and modesty as they can when using a urinal. This needs to be taught in conjunction with learning how to urinate in a urinal.

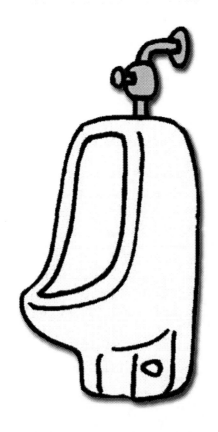

Using A Urinal

⮧ Sometimes when I pee I might use a urinal.

⮧ Everyone who comes into the bathroom can see me when I use the urinal.

⮧ There may be two or more urinals in the bathroom and they won't be inside a stall. It is hard to be private when I use a urinal.

⮧ I need to keep my pants up when I use the urinal.

⮧ I don't drop my pants and underpants when I use the urinal.

⮧ People can see me when I use the urinal. I don't want people to see my butt and I don't want people to see me with no pants on.

⮧ I will be embarrassed and people will be upset to see me with no pants.

⮧ When I use a urinal I must only unzip my pants and open the fly of my underwear to pee.

⮧ I only let my pants drop a little bit. I don't want anyone to see my butt.

⮧

- ☝ Urinals are only for peeing. I can't sit on a urinal. I must stand and face a urinal when I pee.

- ☝ I pee right into the urinal. I will be careful when I pee. I don't splash on the floor. When I'm finished peeing, I flush the urinal.

- ☝ Sometimes when I'm using a urinal someone might be using a urinal next to me.

- ☝ It's not okay to watch someone else use the urinal. It's not okay to look at another person's privates.

- ☝ If someone thinks I am looking at his privates he will be angry and upset. I need to watch my own urinal and pay attention to my own peeing.

- ☝ When I'm finished using the urinal, I will close my fly and zip up my pants.

- ☝ I wash my hands with soap and water before I leave the bathroom.

 I will do a good job using the urinal.